Memory
Palace
MASTER

Dr Gareth Moore B.Sc (Hons) M.Phil Ph.D
is the internationally bestselling author of a wide
range of brain-training and puzzle books for both
children and adults, including *Enigma: Crack the
Code, Ultimate Dot to Dot, Brain Games for Clever
Kids, Lateral Logic* and *Extreme Mazes*. His books
have sold millions of copies in the UK alone,
and have been published in over thirty different
languages. He is also the creator of online brain-
training site BrainedUp.com, and runs the daily
puzzle site PuzzleMix.com.

Find him online at DrGarethMoore.com.

Helena M. Gellersen is a doctoral researcher
in the Memory Laboratory at the University of
Cambridge. Her work centres around long-term
memory and brain changes in healthy ageing and
the early stages of dementia. Her research has
been featured in multiple peer-reviewed journals,
podcasts and blogs.

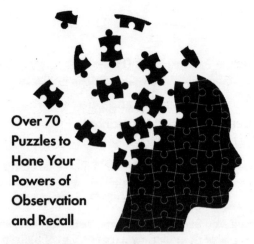

Over 70
Puzzles to
Hone Your
Powers of
Observation
and Recall

Memory Palace MASTER

DR GARETH MOORE

AND HELENA M. GELLERSEN

Michael O'Mara Books Limited

First published in Great Britain in 2021 by
Michael O'Mara Books Limited
9 Lion Yard
Tremadoc Road
London SW4 7NQ

A CIP catalogue record for this book is available from the British Library.

Papers used by Michael O'Mara Books Limited are natural, recyclable products made
from wood grown in sustainable forests. The manufacturing processes conform to the
environmental regulations of the country of origin.

ISBN: 978-1-78929-372-2 in paperback print format

1 2 3 4 5 6 7 8 9 10

Cover design by Jack Smyth
Designed and typeset by Gareth Moore
Chapter 1, and pp. 184-189, include images from Shutterstock.com

Printed and bound by CPI Group (UK) Ltd, Croydon, CR0 4YY

www.mombooks.com

MIX
Paper from
responsible sources
FSC® C020471

Contents

With love to my family and Andrea.
With thanks to Jon Simons and the
Cambridge Memory Lab.
– *Helena M. Gellersen*

INTRODUCTION

The Human Brain

The human brain has long been the subject of great fascination and debate. While Aristotle thought it was just a cooling system for the blood, scientists later realized that the brain is what makes us humans so intelligent. In many regards, though, it is still an enigma. We have succeeded in mapping the entire human genome, the very code that determines the fabric that makes us human, and yet we know relatively little about the complex neural pathways that give rise to all our thoughts.

Nonetheless, in the last century, science has made major strides in our understanding of sensory processes, such as vision and hearing, and cognitive abilities, such as memory. These advances have been hugely influential in showing us how to learn more efficiently. The puzzles in this book have been specially designed using this knowledge about the workings of the human brain to help you acquire strategies to better remember information, both in the short and long term.

It's in our Nature

One of the most fascinating feats of the human brain is its remarkable capacity for committing experiences to memory and learning from them. Computers may beat us at arithmetic or chess but, as yet, there is no system in the known universe that can perform as many different complex tasks with the same degree of sophistication and efficiency as the human brain. Thanks to the billions of cells in your brain – the neurons – and their trillions of connections, it is constantly exchanging myriad signals without us even noticing, allowing us to simultaneously take in information from multiple senses, interact with our friends and colleagues and plan our dinner, and all with seemingly little effort. And by the time we brush our teeth to get ready for bed, we can still bring to mind much of what we did that day.

This ability to remember the past is at the core of our very nature. It allows us to look back and see our current experiences as a logical consequence of what has come before. It gives us a sense of continuity throughout our lives, lets us relive our best and worst experiences and, perhaps most importantly, allows us to build a shared history with those dearest to us. We all know how good it feels to reconnect with an old friend and reminisce about past adventures together. On the other hand, horrible memories of tragic events, such as 9/11, unite people across countries in solidarity and many of us can even remember in detail watching these events unfold. Without our memories, without shared experiences, we would not be able to build bonds with others around us. It is the reason why diseases involving memory loss, such as dementia, are so feared, as they erode these ties we form with others.

What's That Got to Do with Puzzles?

There is not just one type of memory. Rather, memory is multifaceted. Some memories last for a very short period of time and disappear quickly. They may only contain visual information, like an image, or verbal information, like a sentence. Others are rich in detail and extremely vivid. Your memories constitute all the knowledge to which you have access, even if you acquired it decades ago. Importantly, different parts of the brain support different types of memory. For instance, it is the job of some brain regions to retain information for a very short period of time, while others are in charge of remembering it months later.

Given the different memory systems in our brain, it may not be surprising that different strategies are best suited to support, say, long-term memory compared to short-term memory. To help you learn about these strategies, this book has been divided into four key sections. In the first two chapters, you will practise verbal and visual techniques to remember information in the short term. Next, you will practise how to better keep memories in your long-term store so the contents of your short-term memory won't just fade away but can be recalled at a later point in time when needed. The puzzles will gradually become more challenging and by the end of the third chapter you will have learned about a range of strategies to help you retain information. In the final chapter, you will see how these different strategies all work together in a complementary partnership. This is where you take what you have learned to the next level...

Putting It All Together: the Memory Palace

After having completed the short- and long-term memory exercises and hopefully feeling good about what you have learned, you are ready to take the step into the memory palace. This is an ancient technique that is even used by professional 'memory athletes' such as those competing in the World Memory Championships. It is a visualization tool that allows you to build your own mental library of to-be-remembered information by using all the techniques you have honed in the first three chapters and putting them together in one ultimate memory exercise.

At the core of this technique is that old idea that a picture is worth a thousand words, and so using images as building blocks for a mental 'palace' of memories says even more. Essentially, you turn your memories into detailed images that can then be placed into a 3D environment that you can return to whenever you like, mentally walking from one memory to the next. Remarkably, this method dates back to the great Greek poet Simonides more than 2,500 years ago. It was used by many prominent figures in antiquity to help them memorize long speeches and to ensure that they had information readily on hand when needed. So, in completing these puzzles, you will follow in the footsteps of the ancient Greeks.

Working Together in Harmony

Imagine you are listening to an orchestra at a concert. All of the instruments work together in harmony and produce a beautiful symphony. Now imagine you only heard the drums. On its own, the bang of the drums would not be enough for you to even recognize that it is but one part of a grand opus – it only makes sense when heard in concert with the other instruments. Think of your brain as a conductor of such an orchestra: it brings together multiple different types of information – vision, sound, language, emotions – and ultimately binds them together into memories, just like a beautiful symphony. In other words, the whole is more than the sum of its parts. So, who are these different musicians in the brain's orchestra? There are multiple regions across the brain that are in charge of memory processes and you will learn about some of the key players on your journey through this book, such as the hippocampus which can form new, lasting memories, or the prefrontal cortex which maintains information in short-term storage so you can act on it.

The Long of It

Long-term memory is a high-capacity system that can store a massive amount of information. It contains your entire vocabulary and the encyclopedia that holds your knowledge of the world around you, referred to as 'semantic memory'. It allows us to make sense of the world by attaching meaning to what we see, hear and feel. For example, we all know what a chair is and what it is used for. We have developed an abstract concept of what it is and despite the thousands of different designs of chairs that exist, we somehow know that they all represent a variant of the same type of object.

Semantic memory also stores your factual knowledge, such as 'Julius Caesar was a Roman leader' or 'Paris is the capital of France'. It is this type of memory that helps you with crosswords or other types of word puzzle. Though you possess this semantic knowledge, you often don't know where you first learned it. And you don't need to remember

this anyway because, most of the time, the context in which you learned a given fact is not necessary for you to retain that information. This makes facts an excellent target for the memory palace technique, as you can turn them into a single image and place them in your imagined palace: Julius Caesar may become a marble bust on your mantelpiece.

In contrast to semantic memory, 'episodic memory' is rich in context with the when, what, who and where of your life's experiences. Ultimately, it is episodic memory that forms the fabric of our sense of self. It allows us to reminisce; to vividly relive experiences that have long since passed. It weaves together the many scenes, sounds, smells and thoughts that formed an experience, such as eating cake on your last birthday, opening presents at Christmas, you and your friends celebrating graduation, or the first time you met your partner.

Although they work in close collaboration, the regions of the brain that hold our general knowledge and the meaning of words are largely separate from those that allow us to relive past events. Their close collaboration is actually the key to the success of the memory palace technique: the ability of episodic memory systems to bind together pieces of an event into a scene is what we use to build the memory palace and remember the fact that Julius Caesar was a Roman ruler – or even the years when he ruled.

The Short of It

Separate from our massive long-term storage facility, short-term memory is the ability to keep in mind what you just heard, read or saw. Without it, you would be incapable of following the storyline in a book or formulating a coherent thought. You would have already forgotten the last sentence you just read, or even the beginning of this sentence. Information that is held in short-term memory will fade away rapidly in a matter of seconds if it is not used or committed to long-term memory. The capacity of short-term memory is strictly limited. So limited, in fact, that most people will struggle to keep the exact order of more than seven random digits in their mind at any one point in time.

Short-term memory systems can be differentiated based on the type of information that is being retained. Brain areas involved in processing visual information also help keep the identity and location of objects in our environment alive in our mind. Regions that process sounds and the meaning of language support the maintenance of verbal information in short-term memory. Later on, you will see examples of puzzles that test these different types of information

retention. Most importantly, the contents of short-term memory processed by all these regions need to converge to allow you to navigate your surroundings. The connections that exist between these different stores can be used to benefit your short-term memory if you learn how to bring them together to support the same task. For example, it becomes much easier to remember a sequence of numbers when you also imagine the numbers as part of a mental image.

Simply keeping information in temporary storage is not enough, though. We also need to be able to proactively use that information so we can react to our environment. To do this, we organize the information from our short-term store, deciding what deserves our attention and combining pieces from the verbal, visual and spatial systems. This active use of short-term memory contents is termed 'working memory'.

Working memory is one of the functions of our brain that belong to a supervisory system of our behaviour. These 'executive functions' act as 'conductor of the orchestra' – allowing us to control and plan behaviour, flexibly adapt to unfamiliar situations and solve problems. Simply put, working memory is the manager of information kept in your short-term stores. One of the most straightforward examples to demonstrate the contrast between short-term and working memory is the recall of series of numbers: repeating a phone number you've just been given in the same order is a lot less challenging than putting it in reverse order, where your working memory has to move numbers around while remembering the original sequence.

When you are building your memory palace, you engage your working memory to keep multiple different pieces of information actively in your mind – in other words, you decide how to create your palace and choose the images you will use to visualize the information you hope to remember. Your working memory is in charge of putting all of these puzzle pieces together so they can be laid down in your long-term store.

Memory in the Driver's Seat

Looking at each of these types of memory one by one may seem a little abstract. To put it in practical terms, driving is a brilliant example of your short-term and working memory processes as well as your long-term storage system at work.

When you look into your rear-view mirror, the visual system retains a mental image of what was in front of you just before

Executive Functions

Our brains come equipped with a set of mental abilities that are collectively referred to as executive functions, with working memory being just one of those skills in our toolkit. These processes take on a supervisory role and allow us to consciously consider our environment, direct our attention, update our knowledge and adjust our behaviour accordingly. That is not to say that we are not driven by many unconscious processes and that we always act rationally. Rather, we possess the ability to check ourselves, even if we don't always use it!

Although they are supported by a vast network of regions throughout our brains, executive functions are most commonly associated with the prefrontal cortex, the area right behind your forehead. It has expanded significantly throughout the course of human evolution and is larger relative to our total brain size compared to most other animal species. Our executive control brain network is particularly important when we encounter unfamiliar situations and challenging problems, when we need to inhibit certain reactions, when our expectations are violated and when we need to learn new skills.

Whether we solve a maths problem, navigate an unknown public transport system, plan for a new project, resist the temptation to grab for that chocolate bar at the shop or follow a set of complicated (and sometimes seemingly impossible) instructions to build that IKEA bed, executive functions have got you covered. Comprehending and applying all the information in this book about memory strategies will challenge your executive functions but, with more practice, they will soon have to work less hard.

you shifted your attention to what is behind you. All the while, your spatial short-term memory system allows you to remember the positions of all the other objects moving around in your environment. And if your GPS gives you directions, your short-term verbal store is keeping in mind the commands. In contrast, if the route is already familiar to you, your long-term memory store is responsible for navigation. Your working memory uses all that information simultaneously to allow you to react quickly to your environment and plan your movements. And, if something unexpected happens, your executive functions are in charge of taking on that challenge.

Driving may seem like a simple task to many people because it becomes automated through many years of practice but, when we look at all that's involved, it shows how much information the brain has to deal with and how many systems have to work in tandem to orchestrate this complex behaviour that even machines haven't completely mastered (yet). Even though the memory palace method does not require you to actually drive from one place to another, it uses our remarkable capacity for remembering places and getting from point A to point B as the foundation for making lasting memories.

The Big-city Brain

As we have seen in the driving example, all these separate systems need to communicate with one another. At the same time, if all the regions that play a role in memory processes 'talked' to each other non-stop, there would be chaos. Our brains would be like a room full of people at a crowded party: a constant chatter of dozens of voices, from which picking out anything of meaning would be an enormous challenge. The solution to this problem lies in the brain's architecture.

You may imagine the brain as a transport system, similar to the public transport we use in big cities such as London, New York, Tokyo and Berlin. Subregions of the brain have become experts in particular types of tasks that contribute to complex abilities, like movement, vision, planning and short-term or long-term memory. These subregions are not all equally well connected to one another – rather, they form multiple separate specialized networks in which they interact to accomplish these particular functions – just like the different stations grouped along a single train line in a city transport network. And just like people form cohesive social groups and share more information among themselves than with outsiders, so too do different brain regions within their own network.

This architecture makes the brain capable of reducing interference between different types of information, such as visual input and sound, in order to focus and pick out something intelligible from that indistinct party chatter. But this organization also means that if you are confronted with two similar types of input at once, like two people talking at you simultaneously, it will be a challenge to understand both of them. In contrast, when the input is not similar, having different brain networks reduces interference, which is why you usually have no problem talking while driving. You will see that this is particularly important in the case of our fragile short-term memory, where this type of interference between multiple streams of information makes us forget more quickly.

Of course, our brain regions can't be completely isolated from each other or how else would information from the visual and sound systems in the brain be exchanged so you know, for example, that the voice you hear talking belongs to your friend in the passenger seat? The areas that paint a mental image in our brain and those that make meaning of the words we hear can communicate with each other thanks to some brain regions that act as hubs. Hubs are the interfaces between subregions of the brain. You can think of them as major train station interchanges, such as King's

Cross in London or Grand Central station in New York City, which connect different trains or subway lines. Or, to look at it another way, hubs are the life of the party: they always know what's going on with everyone else and they don't mind chatting to people from different friendship groups.

This knowledge about the different functional networks of our brains has helped scientists to better understand why an organ that weighs no more than a medium-size melon is so effective at orchestrating myriad computations into a complex symphony of sensations, movements and thoughts. It is also what forms the basis of this book. Later on, you'll see how one of these hubs will take centre stage as you build your palace. Ultimately, learning new strategies, such as the memory palace method, leads to changes in the communication between brain regions that support memory processes.

Brain Health and Brain Training

Maintaining a healthy brain is a key concern for virtually everyone, especially as we grow older and notice how remembering may become more challenging. There is no single, simple solution to brain health and good memory.

As much as we would all love a spoonful of sugar with the medicine to boost our brain power, or that silver bullet to battle ageing and dementia, the situation is a lot more nuanced than that. Still, there is good news. There are many things we can all do for the good of our brains. Physical exercise, a healthy diet, good sleep, new experiences and social engagement all benefit memory and contribute to keeping us healthy even into old age.

How You Can Train Your Brain

One of the best things you can do to keep cognitively fit is to learn something new. Whoever said that you cannot teach an old dog new tricks was dead wrong! Our brains have great potential for adaptability across our lifespans. Even if learning becomes more difficult as we age, it is still possible to adopt new strategies to help you use your short- and long-term memory capacities more effectively. But for learning to actually work, a few ground rules are key:

1. Being motivated and engaged in a task is vital. This is greatly helped if an exercise is fun, if you are in a good mood when you tackle the exercise and if you can make sure that there are minimal distractions around you.

2. Don't let it get too easy! The brain likes to establish routines that it can use with ease and once a task is not at least a bit challenging any more you have reached a plateau and it's time to move on. This is similar to how you might go to the gym to strengthen muscles and improve endurance, but once your workout starts to feel easy you need to add more weights, run faster or increase your mileage. We will start with basic puzzles so you can get acquainted with the ideas behind memory training and, after you master those, you will gradually complete more difficult puzzles until you are ready to take on the memory palace exercises.

3. Variety is the spice of life and the brain's favourite flavour. Transfer of learned skills from one task to another is the greatest challenge for learning and cognitive training. A general rule is 'what you train is what you get'. You may become highly skilled at crossword puzzles but memorizing new facts may still remain a challenge. So practising with multiple different yet complementary exercises and completing puzzles that require you to learn entirely new strategies is more likely to get you further.

4. Practice takes time. Putting your learning into practice is most important if you hope to see benefits beyond the context of the puzzle. If what you just learned seems easy enough in an exercise, the next step is to apply it in a real-life scenario. From starting small – for instance, by using some of the strategies from these puzzles to complete your grocery shopping without having to look at your list – with practice, you may find that you then use the same techniques in different areas of your everyday life. It may be challenging at first but the brain really is a superior learning machine!

5. Finally, keep the ball rolling! The brain is constantly dealing with new information and we only have limited resources at our disposal. Forgetting is therefore inevitable. When you stop using the knowledge you gained it usually starts to fade away – like the foreign language you may have learned in secondary school but haven't used in years. Refreshers go a long way and will help you to continue reaping the benefits of what you have learned.

Now that you have read about the basics of the brain and its memory systems, hopefully, with each puzzle, you'll realize how that orchestra inside your head – that big-city brain of yours – is working and learning. Exceptional memory skills take enormous practice, or just a very lucky draw in the genetic lottery, but the puzzles in this book will demonstrate how to combine and organize information across different memory systems to help make information stick. And if it ever gets tough, just remember: your brain is made to learn, no matter how old you are! It is up to you to build your palace brick by brick. You may not be able to build it with the high degree of sophistication that memory athletes do but even a small palace is still a palace, and a great place to start!

Helena M. Gellersen

VISUAL MEMORY

Visual Memory

Before you dive right into the memory puzzles, let's get some misconceptions out of the way. Many people are of the firm belief that they simply have a bad memory and that's that. Sure, some people have an outstanding memory and others have far less to work with but memory abilities are not set in stone. Similarly, when we think of ageing and memory, the first thing that often comes to mind is an inevitable decline. But while it is true that ageing affects memory, not everyone experiences significant negative changes as they age. Memory trajectories across our lifespan differ widely between people and so even older adults can benefit from learning new strategies.

If you find yourself subscribing to pessimistic beliefs, you are not giving your ability to positively affect your memory nearly enough credit. Memory is made up of a set of skills – skills that can be developed and worked on. But maybe you already knew that, or why else would you be holding this book right now? In any case, hopefully this reminder will serve as a source of motivation as you get going with the exercises.

Prior to beginning your first exercise, stop and think about a common memory problem that vexes you in your everyday life. Do it now…

If what came to mind was the many times you've forgotten a person's name, you are certainly not alone as this is one of the most common complaints people have. But whatever your answer to the question above, throughout the following chapters, keep your problem in mind and consider how the memory strategies you are trying out in the various exercises may help you next time you are faced with it.

Strategizing

Great mnemonic strategies come down to just a few core concepts: visualization, association, organization and eventually repetition to ensure the maintenance of the contents of your short-term memory store and the formation of truly long-lasting memories. There are multiple ways of successfully committing information to memory and selecting the best method often depends on the type of material – be it visual or verbal, short or long lists of items, or even an entire story or newspaper article. In the following chapters you will practise a variety of techniques to apply to these different situations.

Gone with the Wind

What happens in our environment is fleeting – the world constantly throws new information at us every second of our waking day. Because of our short-term memory, we are able to hold what we just experienced in our minds, even if the physical representation is no longer present in our environment. This ability helps you move from moment to moment while seamlessly connecting your past with your present and your present with your future plans.

We have multiple short-term memory stores for different types of information. The key players you will encounter here are those short-term memory processes in charge of holding visual, verbal and spatial information in your mind. The regions in our brain that process incoming visual stimuli can keep them alive for us even after the image in front of our eyes has disappeared – like remembering what's in front of the car while you look in the rear-view mirror. The same is true for those regions in charge of representing sounds in your mind. This can be likened to an echo of the neural activity that occurred in response to the sound we heard or the image we saw.

Having a short-term store provides the brain with sufficient time to process these sensations, to put them into context and act on them. And as you may remember, manipulating and transforming this information in your mind, as you would while solving a maths problem, relies on your working memory and your executive functions (see box on Executive Functions on page 18). Sadly, we only have finite resources in the face of a constant barrage of signals from our environment and from those that are internally generated by our brains, such as our thoughts and many other unconscious processes beyond. This makes the contents of our short-term memory store extremely fragile.

On Repeat

The most straightforward way of keeping information in our short-term memory alive is through verbal rehearsal. We often use this strategy naturally, for example when someone gives us directions and we repeat the instructions back to them. This kind of articulation keeps contents of our short-term memory 'switched on' to prevent them from decaying; it works for both words and for visual information that you can describe with words.

When we read, hear or see new information, we hardly ever store it just in the form of a visual or as words in our short-term memory – when holding onto images of objects in visual short-term storage we are likely to also have the

corresponding words in our mind. And similarly, when we read a list of words we want to retain in short-term memory, we often form associated images. This use of a dual verbal and visual retention method is a more effective way of storing information than using one of these methods on its own.

You will see that memory for images, for concrete objects that you can label with a single word, is therefore superior to that of more abstract shapes or images that require more words to describe. For example, a sequence of faces or emojis will be more challenging for your short-term memory because you will likely need to create short, distinct descriptors for each one. If you can condense these descriptors by homing in on one unique visual feature and describing it with one or two words instead of multiple ones, however, you can cut down on memory space. An emoji with a squiggly mouth may simply become 'squiggly'. Becoming adept at spotting unique features and using them as a memory anchor can help with these types of tasks. It will also help you later on when you practise how to better remember the names of new people you meet.

In the Spotlight

Let's go back to the example of the indistinct chatter at a party, and how concentration is needed to pick out a particular conversation. Just like at the party, there is a lot of noise in our system from all the constant new sensations, thoughts and other myriad processes in our brains every millisecond of every day. Our attention serves as a pointer to amplify specific contents in our short-term memory, shining a light on a specific piece of information in our limited store while others may fade into the shadows. Information not given some of that spotlight will quickly become inaccessible and forgotten, while that which basks in the limelight can remain live on stage. This is why focusing while in a loud, crowded place is significantly more challenging and why your short-term memory suffers when you try to multitask.

Your executive functions can act as a switch by prioritizing different types of information that are deemed most important for a given task. When you drive and need to concentrate, it can turn down the sounds of the other passengers in the car and focus more on the visuals of your surroundings. When what your co-passengers are saying becomes relevant to your task at hand, for example to navigate to an unfamiliar destination, you can bring the words back into your focus. When people talk about multitasking, what your brain is really doing is just rapid task switching, prioritizing one thing then quickly jumping back to focusing on the other. Effective multitasking is a myth. You may have it all under control but all that switching of attention has a cost and will result in faster decay of the information in your short-term memory. Ultimately, this means that your performance on both tasks will be significantly worse compared to a scenario where you only focused on one at a time.

A good example for the hold your attention has over your short-term memory performance is how much more difficult it is to work in a crowded and buzzing office compared to a quiet environment. With a lot of noise and action going on around you, it is more likely that you will find yourself in the middle of a thought, only to forget what it is you were thinking of after one of the many voices around you diverts your attention, even just for a moment. Setting aside any distractions will serve you well in committing to memory all the knowledge you are acquiring while completing these puzzles.

Making Room

In some of the puzzles in this book, you can test yourself
to determine how many images, words or numbers in a
fixed sequence you can recall from short-term memory. The
number of items you can reliably hold in your mind defines
your short-term memory span. Three to nine pieces is the
normal range for the vast majority of people. But that is not
to say that there aren't ways in which you can enable yourself
to recall even more items. Try to organize the contents of
your short-term memory in such a way that you have fewer
separate items to remember. For example, if you can usually
only manage to recall four items, you could aim to condense
eight items into four separate pictures in your mind and
suddenly the total number of items that stick in your short-
term memory may double.

Fusing pieces of information together means that you can
free up resources for other items, or chunks, to comfortably
fit within your limited short-term memory. In other words,
the 'chunking' mnemonic strategy – whereby multiple 'items'
are combined into a single 'item' – allows you to use your
own short-term memory span more efficiently. In fact, this is
the key to all the memory training exercises in these puzzles
– to become better at working with the resources you already
have at your disposal. People who use this technique are

capable of engaging their working memory processes more effectively.

Let Me Paint You a Picture

Humans crucially rely on vision more than all other senses to orient themselves in the world. We have no problem recalling thousands of objects or entire scenes rich with detail from memory and most of us can create new pictures in our minds with ease. In fact, visual information often has an advantage over verbal material, written or spoken, which is why almost all effective mnemonic strategies involve some kind of visualization.

You can improve your chunking technique by painting a memorable mental picture that you can populate with many items at once. This can be done by choosing an overarching framework in which you put items in context with each other. This improves your chances that by recalling one of the items the others may then follow. For example, if you wanted to build a scene to help you remember the items 'tree', 'chair', 'leash', 'apple' and 'moon', you may choose the tree as the central item around which to position the others. The apple naturally finds a place on the tree. The leash may be draped around the branches like decorative Christmas lights. The chair may lean against the tree trunk and the whole scene is bathed in moonlight.

Conjuring up such images may be challenging at first but, with practice, you will soon be able to paint such unusual and memorable scenes in your mind. Throughout this book, you will encounter a variety of these visualization techniques to use as mnemonic aids. You will soon see that your imagination is truly an artist when it comes to supporting both short- and long-term memory.

1.1: Ordered Pictures

Start by covering over the bottom half of this page. Then take a look at these six pictures. Try to memorize the order they are in. Once you are happy you'll recall the same ordering, uncover the bottom half of the page and cover over the top half instead.

Can you recall the order these images were in originally? Draw lines linking each image to the box corresponding to its original position in the arrangement above.

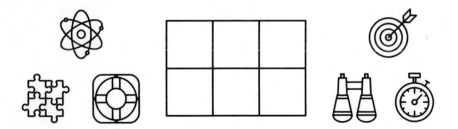

1.2: More Ordered Pictures

Repeat the previous exercise, but this time with the larger set of images shown below. Spend no more than about 30 seconds memorizing their arrangement.

Can you recall the order these images were in originally? Draw lines linking each image to the box corresponding to its original position in the arrangement above.

1.3: At a Glance

Start by covering over the bottom half of this page. Then take a quick look at the six pictures below, but cover them over after about 15 seconds. Then cover the top half of the page and reveal the text below.

Draw lines linking each image to the box corresponding to its original position in the arrangement above.

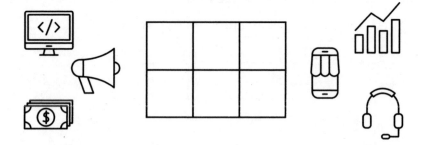

Did you find this exercise any harder when you did not have as much time to memorize the ordering first?

1.4: Draw It Again

Study the pattern at the top of the page for as long as you wish, then cover it over and try to reproduce it as accurately as you can on the grid beneath.

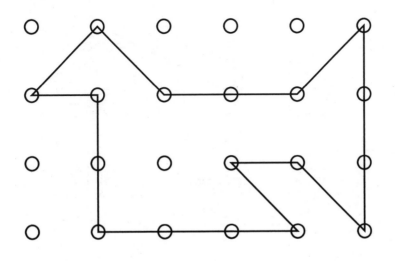

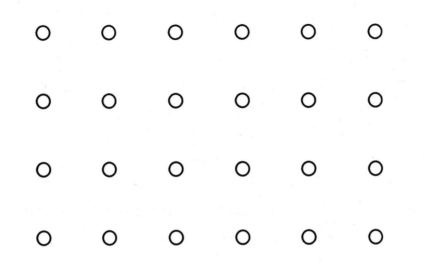

1.5: Draw This Again Too

Study the pattern at the top of the page for as long as you wish, then cover it over and try to reproduce it as accurately as you can on the grid beneath.

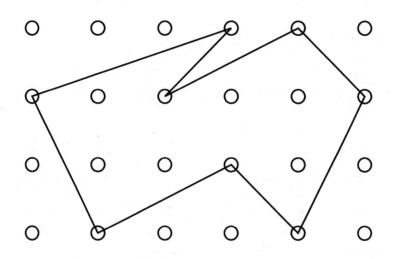

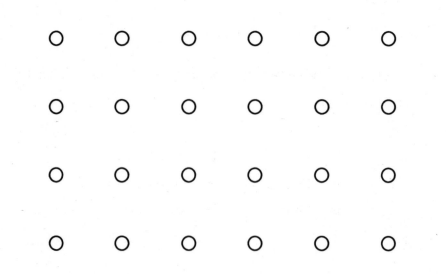

1.6: Image Association

Each picture below is associated with a word. Study the pictures and words, and try to memorize the associations. Once you think you are ready, cover them over and then see if you can link the original accompanying word to the correct image below. The list of words will be given.

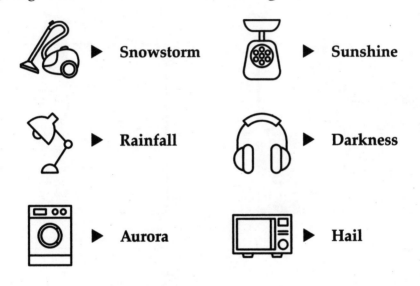

Cover over the above before attaching each of these words to the correct image:

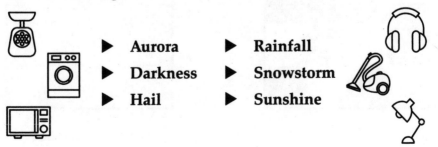

▶ Aurora ▶ Rainfall

▶ Darkness ▶ Snowstorm

▶ Hail ▶ Sunshine

1.7: Grid Memory

Look at the pattern in the grid on the left of the page, then cover it over and see if you can accurately reproduce it in the empty grid on the right of the page. Repeat similarly for each of the four exercises.

Exercise 1

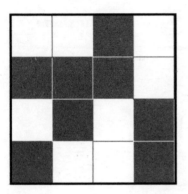 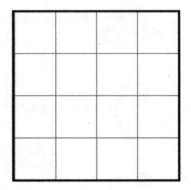

Exercise 2

 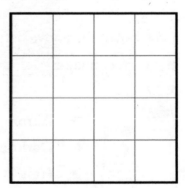

Exercise 3

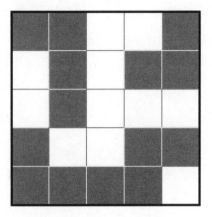 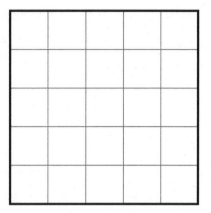

Exercise 4

1.8: Facing Up

Look at each of these emojis in turn, then cover them over and see how accurately you can redraw them on the empty circles below.

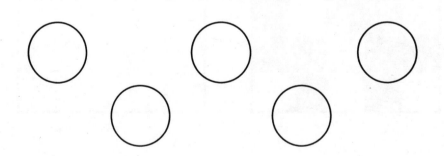

1.9: Drawing a Blank

Draw six emojis of your choice, perhaps using the pictures opposite for inspiration, then cover them over and see how accurately you can redraw them on the empty circles at the bottom of this page.

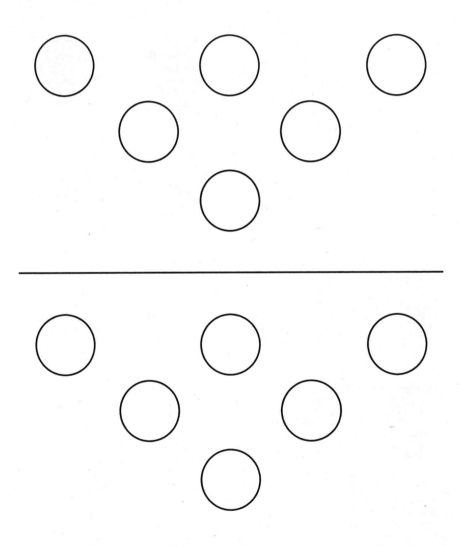

1.10: Picture Arrangement

Cover over the page to the right. Then, test your memory by studying this arrangement of environmentally related images below. After no more than 60 seconds looking at it, cover it over and reveal the question on the opposite page.

Beneath you can see some – but not all – of the same environmentally related images, which are otherwise in the same arrangement. Can you circle all of the images which have changed?

1.11: Shape Grid

First, cover over the bottom half of the page. Next, pay attention to help you try to memorize the arrangement of the shapes in the grid below. Once ready, continue below.

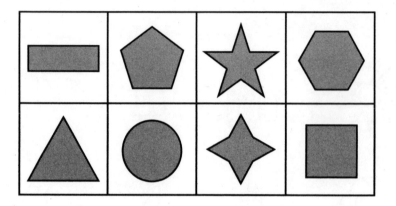

Now cover over the top half of the page instead. Can you restore all of the shapes to the empty grid below?

1.12: Picture Descriptions

Spend a few minutes looking at the following pictures, then cover them over and write out descriptions of as many of the images as you can recall on a blank sheet of paper.

1.13: Names and Faces

Study the names attached to each of the faces on this page, and attempt to memorize which name belongs to which face. Spend as long as you like on this, then when you are ready cover over the image and continue on the opposite page.

Daphne

Sanjid

Simona

Andreas

Gayatri

Can you write the correct name of each person underneath their corresponding face below?

....

....

....

....

....

1.14: Tougher Drawing

Study the pattern at the top of the page for as long as you wish, then cover it over and try to reproduce it as accurately as you can on the grid beneath.

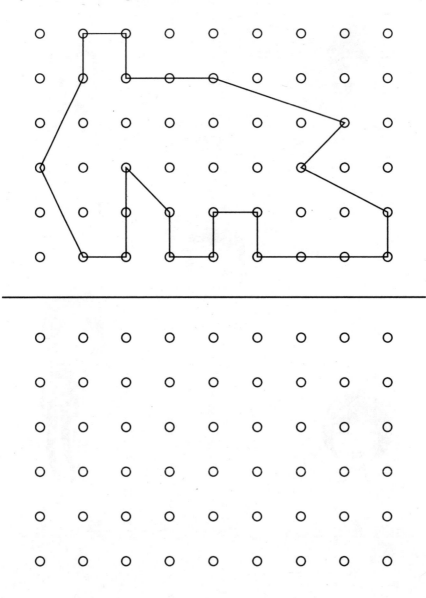

1.15: Road Route

Try to memorize the route that this road takes, then cover it over and try to recreate it on the empty grid below.

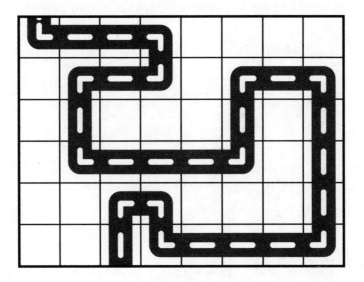

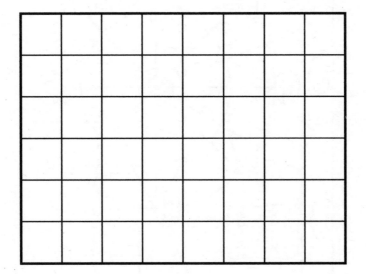

1.16: Remember the Difference

Cover the page opposite, then spend as long as you like studying this image below, rotating the page first. When ready, cover this page instead and reveal the opposite page.

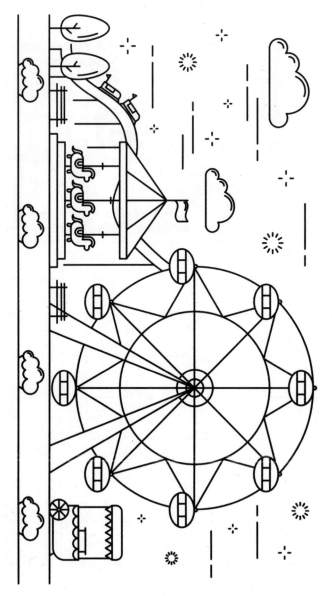

Can you spot all eight objects which have vanished? None of the lines in the sky or stars have been removed – only major objects. Rotate the image first before examining it.

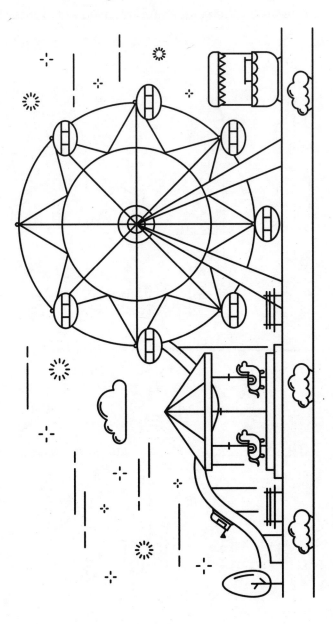

1.17: Added Images

Cover the bottom half of the page, then study the top half. Once 60 seconds is up, reveal the bottom and cover the top. Can you circle all of the images which are new? Note that the images may be in a different location to when first given.

1.18: Vanished Images

Cover the bottom half of the page, then study the top half. Once 60 seconds is up, reveal the bottom and cover the top. Can you use a blank piece of paper to write a description of all of the images which have vanished? Note that the images may be in a different location to when first given.

VERBAL MEMORY

Verbal Memory

Language is key to our understanding of the world around us. We use it constantly to form plans and solve problems in our mind. Verbal working memory allows you to retain and manipulate verbal information, whether heard, spoken or read, for a short period of time. It is this system that helps you keep in mind the first part of this sentence while you read on so you can make sense of its meaning. In the previous chapter, you took your first steps to learn about key concepts for effective mnemonic strategies. Next, you can practise these methods on verbal material.

On a Loop

Verbal material readily lends itself to rehearsal, which is the primary means by which we keep this information in mind. Active rehearsal has its limits, though, because the longer the sequence of words becomes, the longer it takes to repeat. At some point, rehearsal will take so long that, by the time you reach the final item on the list, the first has slipped your mind. This is why you can recall more items from a list when words are short ('pin', 'car', 'cat') compared to a list with longer words ('banana', 'fire engine', 'caterpillar'). The shorter words are also more likely to be remembered. Mandarin speakers have on average a greater short-term memory for numbers because the words describing each number are generally shorter than those in English. To overcome limitations of our short-term memory span, the chunking method that we discussed previously – and which hopefully you have now practised – lends itself equally well to the material you are tasked to recall in these exercises.

Connecting the Dots

You can group more items in your memory if you provide a logical framework. Putting items in context with each other strengthens the associations between them and thereby the chances that recalling one of them means that the others will follow. Let us return to an example from the previous chapter: the list containing 'tree', 'chair', 'leash', 'apple' and 'moon'. Here, all items were combined into one picture but the order in which one recalled them was irrelevant. If, however, it is vital to remember the exact order, this can be achieved by transforming the words into a sequence of events in which items are linked sequentially. This link system requires you to connect one item after the other by conjuring up an interaction between each successive pair. The more dynamic this interaction, the better. You could begin with a tree that, sadly, is chopped up and provides the wood for a chair, which in turn is pulled by a leash until it falls to the ground. Next, the leash is used to hurl the apple into the sky, where the fruit magically turns into the celestial body that is the moon. These may all be very fanciful images but that is exactly why they are so effective!

Tell Me a Story

Instead of these relatively abstract associations between single items in your memory, you could instead group information by telling yourself a story that places all of the items into a cohesive narrative. This method is most appropriate for cases in which items are at least somewhat related to each other. An advantage of the story mnemonic is that you may not even need to create elaborate mental images of the events in the story.

To give yourself a starting point, you might like to use elements of a story you already know. Because narratives have a logical structure where one event follows another, this method lends itself to the recall of a fixed sequence of items. The story mnemonic is also relatively robust to the forgetting of a single item. Because the story provides one overarching framework, you can jump ahead to the next item without getting caught up by having forgotten a single item in the chain. This is an advantage over the link method where forgetting one item can have a more detrimental effect on the recall of others. You may question the practical use of memorizing a list of random words, but the point of such an exercise is to get your creative juices flowing – which will ultimately serve in the construction of your memory palace.

Throw Me a Lifeline

Recalling a series of words from your short-term memory may be easier for you than doing the same for a series of numbers. This is because you have intuitively formed pictures of the meaning of these words or you may have actively tried to make associations between them, as laid out in the examples above. A more advanced technique to the ones we have already discussed is known as the 'peg mnemonic'. This technique combines visualization and association and allows you to recall numbers or items from a list. You can think of pegs as hooks on which you can 'hang' information that you wish to remember. Here, we will use a rhyming peg to represent different numbers.

Before this technique is of any use to you, you need to create your pegs. Here we are going to use rhymes. For each number 0 to 10, pick one word that rhymes with it – one may be a gun, two is a shoe, three is a tree, four = door, five = hive, six = sticks, seven = heaven, eight = weight, nine = wine, ten = hen, nil = hill. You then use the link system together with your pegs to make associations between all the rhyming words that represent the corresponding numbers.

So for 191027, you may think of a gun that goes off to shoot a glass of wine, which then spills onto the ground. Next, a hen drinks the spilled wine and becomes so inebriated that it falls asleep in an old shoe while dreaming of heaven. The peg method can even help you when recalling this same sequence in backwards order. This mnemonic technique will require some time investment but once the pegs are placed firmly in your memory, recalling long number sequences will be substantially easier.

Alliance Against Forgetting

Short-term and long-term memory do not act in isolation. They are partners in crime and lend each other a helping hand in the fight against forgetting. When you are bringing long-term memories back from their store into your active mind, you are keeping their contents in short-term memory. Conversely, relevant information from short-term memory can be transferred to your long-term storage. In fact, by having used all of the mnemonic techniques in these first two chapters, you will have increased your chances of successful short- to long-term transfer.

You can use what you have saved in your long-term store to guide the organization of the contents in short-term memory. Professional chess players do this constantly when they plan

ten steps ahead in their working memory to outsmart their
opponent. They are trained to recognize common patterns
on the board that they can organize into larger chunks which
contain multiple chess pieces. What is fascinating is that they
can only employ this strategy when the configuration of the
chess pieces reflects a plausible combination of positions
that occurs in a real game and not if the pieces are randomly
organized.

The chess example shows how long-term memory can be
your most faithful ally in keeping items in short-term store
alive in your mind. If you were presented with a random
list of digits such as 8137004 and your birthday was on the
13 July, you would already have one chunk that consists of
three numbers in the sequence, 137. The same method works
for letters. Wherever you can assign meaning to these types
of sequences, you can significantly reduce the load working
memory has to carry and increase your chances of long-term
memory retention.

Difficulty

The tasks on the following pages may sometimes have more
entries than you are comfortable memorizing. If so, just
shorten them until you are happy with the exercise. You can
always return and try the full list at some point later.

2.1: Digital Recollection

Spend up to 30 seconds memorizing each sequence of digits given below, then cover them over and see how accurately you can recall them in the space given. For the later exercises, you'll be asked to recall the digits in different orders to those given – but you should memorize them in the original order.

Exercise 1

1 7 3 6 8 4

Recall the six digits:

....

Exercise 2

9 4 3 8 7 1 2

Recall the seven digits:

....

Exercise 3

9 4 1 8 3 6

Recall the six digits in reverse order to that given:

....

Exercise 4

5 8 3 5 4 3 7

Recall the seven digits in reverse order to that given:

....

Exercise 5

9 3 4 6 2 1 4 5

Recall the eight digits in increasing order of value:

....

2.2: Simple Lists

Spend 30 seconds memorizing the list of words below, then cover them over and read the instructions beneath the line:

Hamster

Roof

Cheese

Doctor

Rainbow

Excitement

Now you have covered them over, see if you can number the same words in the order they were given above, writing '1' for the first word in the list, '2' for the second word in the list, and so on up to '6' for the final item.

....	**Rainbow**
....	**Hamster**
....	**Excitement**
....	**Doctor**
....	**Roof**
....	**Cheese**

2.3: Detailed Lists

Study this list of films and directors that won the Oscar for 'Best Picture', then cover them over and see how many you can recall when only the directors and dates are given.

2000: *Gladiator*, Ridley Scott

2001: *A Beautiful Mind*, Ron Howard

2002: *Chicago*, Rob Marshall

2003: *The Lord of the Rings: The Return of the King*, Peter Jackson

2004: *Million Dollar Baby*, Clint Eastwood

Now see if you can fill in the gaps:

2000: ...., **Ridley Scott**

2001: ...., **Ron Howard**

2002: ...., **Rob Marshall**

2003: ...., **Peter Jackson**

2004: ...., **Clint Eastwood**

2.4: PIN Codes

Study this list of four-digit PIN codes for one or two minutes, then cover them over and see if you can recall the missing information at the bottom of the page:

Apartment keypad:	**5720**
Office:	**3957**
Phone unlock:	**8374**
ATM PIN:	**7112**

Can you fill in the gaps? Note that the list is in a different order to before.

Phone unlock:	....
ATM PIN:	....
....**:**	**5720**
Office:	....

2.5: Passwords

Now you have tried PIN codes, try this trickier list of passwords to memorize. Study the list for two minutes, then cover it up, read the prompt and fill in the gaps below.

Office email:	**NorthWestXYZ**
Bank account:	**MON£Y$AFE**
Electricity bill:	**GREEN247**
Online groceries:	**ShopDrop84**
Social media:	**ZXCVBNM**
Family photos:	**2021TeamHeston**

Can you complete the missing information? Note that the list is in a different order to before.

Electricity bill: ....

....: **2021TeamHeston**

Bank account: ....

....: **ShopDrop84**

Social media: ....

Office email: ....

2.6: Longer Lists

Look at the following list of English counties, and take note of the (arbitrary) order they are listed in. When you're ready, cover them over and write the original list position number next to each of the counties on the unnumbered, differently ordered list on the opposite page.

1. **Durham**

2. **Gloucestershire**

3. **Kent**

4. **Somerset**

5. **Rutland**

6. **Devon**

7. **Cheshire**

8. **Norfolk**

9. **Essex**

10. **Cumbria**

11. **Northumberland**

12. **Bedfordshire**

13. **North Yorkshire**

14. **Surrey**

15. **Cornwall**

16. **Suffolk**

Having covered over the list opposite, see if you can write the original list number next to each of the following counties. They are given in a different order to before. (If this task is too hard, try starting with just six or eight counties and then build up until you can memorize the order of all sixteen).

.... : **Northumberland**

.... : **Cheshire**

.... : **Durham**

.... : **Cornwall**

.... : **Gloucestershire**

.... : **Essex**

.... : **Kent**

.... : **Suffolk**

.... : **Somerset**

.... : **North Yorkshire**

.... : **Devon**

.... : **Norfolk**

.... : **Bedfordshire**

.... : **Surrey**

.... : **Rutland**

.... : **Cumbria**

2.7: Crazy Connections

To memorize the shopping list of items below, see if you can think of a humorous way to connect them all – perhaps by inventing a short story which involves each of the items in turn. When you're ready, cover up the list and fill in the gaps on the opposite page with the list of items in the same order, using your new creative memory tool to help you.

Shampoo

Soap

Sweetcorn

Salami

Salmon

Squash

Scissors

Sunscreen

Salad

Soda

Sardines

Sausages

Soup

Spaghetti

After you have covered up the opposite page, see if you can recall your shopping list in the same order it was given by using your memorable connections.

....

....

....

....

....

....

....

....

....

....

....

....

....

2.8: Joking Around

Take a look at this list of jokes, and see how many you can learn in just two minutes. When time is up, cover them over and follow the instructions on the opposite page.

Why didn't the pony sing in the choir?
Because it was a little horse.

What did the sea say to the shore?
Nothing, it just waved.

What did '0' say to '8'?
Nice belt.

Why didn't the skeleton go to the ball?
Because he had no body to go with.

Where's the best place to learn about ice cream?
Sundae school.

Why can't a nose be twelve inches long?
Because it would be a foot.

Why are teddy bears never hungry?
Because they're always stuffed.

See if you can fill in the gaps below. And try them out on family and friends over the next few days!

Why can't a nose be twelve inches long?

....

Why didn't the pony sing in the choir?

....

....

Because they're always stuffed.

....

Nothing, it just waved.

....

Because he had no body to go with.

What did '0' say to '8'?

....

Where's the best place to learn about ice cream?

....

2.9: Chemical Callback

The periodic table displays all of the known chemical elements which make up the natural world, ordered by atomic number. Eight of those elements are given below, along with the year they were first formally observed or predicted.

Phosphorous:	**1669**
Cobalt:	**1735**
Platinum:	**1735**
Nickel:	**1751**
Magnesium:	**1755**
Hydrogen:	**1766**
Oxygen:	**1771**
Barium:	**1772**

Study this list of elements for a few minutes, and see if you can memorize both the list of elements and also the associated year that each was first observed.

Once you're confident you can remember them, cover up the elements and follow the instructions on the opposite page.

Once you have covered up the previous page, see if you can fill in the gaps below with the information you have memorized:

Phosphorous: ....

....: **1735**

Platinum: ....

....: **1751**

Magnesium: ....

....: **1766**

Oxygen: ....

....: **1772**

Try returning to the list in an hour, and then tomorrow, the day after, and even a few days after that. Can you still remember them?

2.10: Passage Recall

Read the following passage a few times to memorize the basic facts. Once you feel that you're ready, cover the text and see if you can answer the recall questions opposite.

Leonardo da Vinci was a Renaissance polymath whose talents straddled the worlds of art and science. He was born in Italy, near to modern-day Florence, in 1452.

Even in his own time he was a highly celebrated painter; his most recognizable painted works are *The Mona Lisa* and *The Last Supper*. He was also interested in anatomy and created several highly accurate sketches of the human body. His drawing *The Vitruvian Man*, showing an outstretched human figure, was created around 1490, and is currently on display in a gallery in Venice.

Da Vinci was also an engineer, and created early prototypes for flying machines, parachutes and even a mechanical knight known as 'Leonardo's Robot'. He spent most of his life in Italy, though he lived in France for the last three years of his life, until his death in 1519.

Now see if you can answer the following questions, without checking back to the passage on the previous page:

1. In what year was da Vinci born?

2. Which word, meaning 'a widely learned person', was used to describe da Vinci in the first paragraph?

3. Which two paintings are named in the passage as da Vinci's most famous?

4. In which country did da Vinci spend the last three years of his life?

5. Which three inventions mentioned in the text is it said that da Vinci created prototypes of?

6. Near what modern Italian city was da Vinci born?

7. In approximately what did year did da Vinci draw *The Vitruvian Man*?

8. In what city is *The Vitruvian Man* currently displayed?

9. In what year did da Vinci die?

2.11: Spot the Difference

Closely read the following excerpt from *Pride and Prejudice* by Jane Austen, and then follow the instructions opposite:

It is a truth universally acknowledged, that a single man in possession of a good fortune, must be in want of a wife.

However little known the feelings or views of such a man may be on his first entering a neighbourhood, this truth is so well fixed in the minds of the surrounding families, that he is considered the rightful property of some one or other of their daughters.

"My dear Mr. Bennet," said his lady to him one day, "have you heard that Netherfield Park is let at last?"

Mr. Bennet replied that he had not.

"But it is," returned she; "for Mrs. Long has just been here, and she told me all about it."

Mr. Bennet made no answer.

"Do you not want to know who has taken it?" cried his wife impatiently.

"You want to tell me, and I have no objection to hearing it."

This was invitation enough.

Cover the passage on the previous page, then read this very similar passage – which has had ten words changed. Can you find them all? The solution, if needed, is on page 190.

It is a truth universally acknowledged, that a man in possession of a great fortune, must be in want of a wife.

However little known the feelings or views of such a man may be on his first entering a community, this truth is so well fixed in the minds of the surrounding families, that he is considered the rightful property of some one or other of their daughters.

"My dear Mr. Bennet," said his lady to him yesterday, "have you heard that Mansfield Park is let at last?"

Mr. Bennet replied that he had not.

"But it is," returned she; "for Mrs. Short has just been here, and she told me all about it."

Mr. Bennet made no reply.

"Do you not want to know who has taken it?" cried his wife eagerly.

"You mean to tell me, and I have no objection to hearing it."

This was encouragement enough.

2.12: Wondrous Words

Spend two minutes studying this list of words of Japanese origin. They have not been sorted into any particular order.

When the time is up, cover the list and follow the instructions on the opposite page:

KARATE

TERIYAKI

BONSAI

KIMONO

TSUNAMI

HAIKU

TYCOON

KABUKI

SUDOKU

WASABI

SATSUMA

KARAOKE

KAMIKAZE

MANGA

ORIGAMI

Make sure you have covered the list on the previous page. Now can you rewrite the list of words of Japanese origin in the spaces below, in any order you like?

....

....

....

....

....

....

....

....

....

....

....

....

....

2.13: To-do List

Read this list of things you might need to remember to do, and spend a few minutes memorizing it. When you're done, cover it up and read the instructions beneath:

Groceries

Pick up Grandpa

Pay water bill

Fix broken shelves

Water the plants

Mow the lawn

Buy printer paper

Clean fridge drawers

Defrost dinner

Fold laundry

Change light bulbs

Walk the dog

Call Mum

Once you have covered up the list above, see if you can recall each of the items on it. The first letter from each line has been given below, in alphabetical order, as an aide-memoire:

B C C C D F F G M P P W W

2.14: The Power of Poetry

Spend one minute studying this limerick by Edward Lear. When the time is up, cover it up and follow the instructions beneath:

There was an Old Man with a beard,

Who said, 'It is just as I feared!'

Two Owls and a Hen, Four Larks and a Wren,

Have all built their nests in my beard!

Now see if you can rewrite the poem on the lines below, without referring back to the original. Try to get the words exactly the same, but don't worry about the punctuation.

....

....

....

....

2.15: Test Your Memory

How closely have you been paying attention throughout this chapter? Each of the following questions relates to one of the memory exercises in the previous pages. See how many you can answer without looking back at the original exercises – and find out which memories have stuck! If you need them, solutions can be found on page 190.

1. In which country was Leonardo da Vinci born?

2. In what year was barium first observed?

3. Which two people were talking in the excerpt from *Pride and Prejudice*?

4. What was the PIN code for the bank ATM?

5. What did '0' say to '8'?

6. Which of these did **not** appear in the list of English counties?
   - ▶ North Yorkshire
   - ▶ Durham
   - ▶ Dorset

7. Which film won the Oscar for Best Picture in 2000?

8. Who directed *Million Dollar Baby*?

9. What was the password for the electricity bill?

10. How many birds nested in the man's beard, in total, in Edward Lear's limerick?

11. Which joke had the punchline 'Because it would be a foot'?

12. Which eight chemical elements were listed, and what were their years of discovery?

Once you've answered these questions, you could try the following bonus challenges, writing your answers on blank sheets of paper:

▶ **Write out as many of the words of Japanese origin as you can recall.**
▶ **Write out as many of the items beginning with 'S' as you can remember from the silly story you invented.**
▶ **Which items from the to-do list can you remember?**

LONG-TERM
MEMORY

Long-term Memory

The healthy brain can store vast amounts of information, as shown by the seemingly impossible abilities of memory grand masters, who can remember 1,000 random digits in under an hour, or savants such as Kim Peek, the real-life inspiration for the movie *Rain Man*, who committed much of the contents of his local library to memory. Our long-term memory stores hold the essential information needed to make sense of the world around us, use language, connect with other people, access a repertoire of skills and navigate our surroundings. As we have seen, these abilities are supported by different memory systems that work together (also see 'Getting to Know Patient HM' on page 101).

The processes supporting memorization are known as encoding, storage and retrieval. During encoding, your brain transfers your experiences of an event or a new fact into the memory system. This process can be automatic or effortful, in that you can influence what you remember later by focusing on specific aspects that you find important. In the following exercises, you should practise using encoding strategies to help increase the likelihood that you can retrieve the memory later on. For long-term retention, the encoded information has to be stored so that it can be accessed at a later point in time. And, finally, to bring back a memory to mind it needs

to be retrieved. Again, this can happen seamlessly without you even trying or you may have to strategically search your mind to find a specific piece of information you need. With just the right technique, this search can be made a lot easier.

That's My Cue

On your own you may not be able to remember details of your friend's birthday celebration last year but then when they reminisce about the great gifts they received you may suddenly recall the blue wrapping paper you used for their present. This is the fundamental difference between free recall, where you require no reminders, and cued recall where prompts act as keys to those drawers of your filing cabinet where your memories lie dormant.

Learning how to make effective cues for yourself is incredibly helpful for remembering a variety of information – particularly facts, vocabulary or short lists. A cue could be as simple as a single first letter of a word, or it could be an acronym like the SOH CAH TOA rules you learned in trigonometry to help you remember that sine equals the opposite over the hypothenuse in a triangle. It could have a certain rhythmical nature, such as 'divorced, beheaded, died; divorced, beheaded, survived' for the six wives of Henry VIII, or 'in fourteen hundred and ninety-two, Columbus

sailed the ocean blue' for an important date. These cues give you a starting point for where to search your memory and, if they become sufficiently engrained, they can automatically trigger your brain to bring back the information you need.

Use What You Know

Memories do not exist in a vacuum. Our brains are geared towards building a mental map of the world around us that we can use to guide our behaviour flexibly. We have built memory structures containing our knowledge of our social network, facts and language; we've formed maps of our surroundings to help us navigate; and we have a rich tapestry of personal history woven into a coherent image of who we are. We can use this substantial knowledge at our disposal to anchor new pieces of information to old ones. This allows us to make new connections with content that is already stable in our memory.

A Scaffold for Your Memories

When you hope to successfully store a larger amount of information in your memory, such as multiple facts related to a common topic or a story, structuring the content is key. As we have seen above, this will be a lot easier when an anchor to your prior knowledge is readily available but, if the information is new, developing a scaffold is more of a challenge. For example, you may choose a single word or picture to represent the core theme and organize other pieces of information around it like the spokes of a wheel. This is particularly helpful if you are hoping to increase your general knowledge of a new topic. Similarly, when you have a list of items, for instance groceries you need to buy, you can group the items by category to decrease the number of unique pieces on the list. If you are hoping to recall a sequence of events or items that have a temporal order, picking out one word to represent each piece and linking them together is the better strategy. You can then use one of the mnemonic methods discussed in previous chapters to strengthen your cues.

Put It on a Canvas

You have already learned how our abilities to paint a mental picture give us a powerful tool to encode information in a way that makes recall substantially easier. For these long-term memory puzzles, you can form a picture or even an entire scene in your mind. Really elaborate on the information that you hope to recall. For example, when you are learning about historical facts, painting a mental image of a given event and embellishing it will help you remember.

This also works for abstract knowledge such as new words. For 'ignominious' (dishonourable, disgraceful) you could imagine an evil little gnome letting out an ominous laugh.

One reason this is so effective is that a picture, more so than words, can be bound into one unique representation of what you hope to remember. The method reduces interference from unimportant memories or new incoming information. As you have seen, one piece of the puzzle can act as a cue, which may be enough to trigger your brain to bring back the memory in all its colours, so having multiple potential memory traces contained in a rich and detailed image will boost your chances of recall.

Putting Together One and One

You have already seen how linking different pieces of information can aid your short-term memory in retaining lists of items. Your long-term memory is a master in forging these types of associations. In terms of your knowledge of the world, you know that bread and butter go together and that thunder follows lightning. When you see a corgi, you may think of the Queen. And when it comes to your own personal history, a particular song or a smell may be tightly linked to a particular memory. By making a conscious effort, you can leverage this ability to improve recall. For example,

when you hope to remember someone's name, you could try finding a prominent facial feature that you could tie to the name. If Irene has particularly blue eyes, she becomes Eye-rene. Alternatively, you could also associate the name of someone you just met with someone you already know, be it a friend or a famous person.

In a previous chapter, we talked about a classic mnemonic technique called the peg method and its use for memorizing sequences of numbers. Now you can practise the peg method for objects that represent a given number. This will allow you to choose whether you prefer a rhyming peg or a visual one. The shape of the objects that you pick as your new pegs should be reminiscent of the shape of their corresponding number: one may be a pen, two could be a swan, three could be the humps of a camel, and so on. After choosing these pegs you can 'hang' information on them that you wish to recall, such as your to-do list for the day. For example, 1) writing an important email – this could be an image of you hitting the keys with a pen; 2) buying a birthday present for your friend – this could be a swan cradling a wrapped present in its nest; 3) getting the car fixed – this could be a camel that is trying to pull a broken car. Once you have etched your pegs into your mind you can reuse them time and time again. By having fixed pegs that require no conscious effort to recall, you have given yourself a go-to cue that you can reuse when you need to quickly memorize a list of new items.

Here to Stay

Most of what we experience every day will be forgotten at some point. The process of proofing a memory against forgetting is called consolidation. This is where the connections between neurons that make up a given memory are being strengthened. Over time, memories that are recalled repeatedly become more and more consolidated until they are here to stay. As you may have discovered with some of these puzzles, spacing out your learning over several days or even weeks will make remembering easier and easier each time. Nonetheless, if you let memories sit unused for years, they become weakened until they can no longer be retrieved. This is probably the fate of a lot of what you learned in school, even if you aced the exams back then. A quick refresher every once in a while may be but a small price to pay to keep your hard-earned knowledge accessible.

Getting to Know Patient HM

The distinctions between our various long-term memory systems are best exemplified by the story of Henry Molaison, originally only known as Patient HM. Back when the treatment for debilitating epilepsy was less sophisticated, doctors took a radical step to stop Henry's seizures for good: they removed in each half of the brain the region that was responsible for his condition. This structure is the hippocampus, named after the Greek word for 'seahorse' because its shape vaguely resembles that of the marine animal.

After the surgery, doctors soon realized that they had to reintroduce themselves to HM time and time again. Although Henry knew who he was and remembered much of his earlier life, he could no longer form new conscious memories of his experiences after the surgery, meaning his episodic memory was severely impaired. He was, however, capable of learning new complex motor skills, even though he was unable to remember having learned them in the first place – so his procedural memory, which supports the acquisition of skills, was intact. His command of language was unchanged and, to his death, Henry was also an avid crossword puzzler – but with the caveat that he could not answer any questions with clues referring to events after his surgery. His semantic memory for language and facts he already knew worked well but again, novel information did not stick.

This seemingly bizarre pattern of memory impairment and preservation shows that the hippocampus is the key player in making new lasting memories. It is this region that you will engage when taking on the puzzles in this chapter.

Sleep on it

One of the best things you can do to support memory consolidation is to sleep. While you sleep, your brain is hard at work making the neurons that were active during an event you recently experienced replay those previous patterns of activity. You can think of it as fast-forwarding through a movie of what happened to you that day, but it takes place without you even noticing. Reviewing what you hope to learn right before you go to bed is particularly effective because it is still fresh in your mind and less impacted by interfering information you encountered throughout the day.

Coming Back Around

If you have made it this far, you have already spent a considerable amount of time on these memory exercises. Such an investment should not be for naught. After all, you don't just want to get good at memory puzzles. You want to take your practice home with you, so to speak. You have made a great start and now it is time to challenge yourself even further by applying these techniques to all sorts of scenarios in day-to-day life.

Now that you have had a chance to learn about mnemonic strategies, take some time to consider your memorization techniques once more and let's see if you can get on the right PATH for future memorization by using the following steps:

▶ First define your problem (P), which you have already done at the beginning of your memory journey.

▶ The second step is to analyse (A) its components. For instance, in the face-name example you can note that you have two pieces of information and your goal is to associate the two so next time you don't just recognize that face but can also greet the other person with their name.

▶ Now consider the different techniques (T) you have been practising so far throughout this book.

▶ Selecting the right mnemonic technique will help (H) you next time you are facing that situation.

By considering everyday scenarios and applying the PATH framework, you are taking a step away from the confines of these pages and bracing yourself to face real-life memory puzzles. Yes, it takes time to use mnemonics to encode information but, once you've done it, retrieving information you need will be quicker and your memories will be more protected from forgetting. Don't give up if you do not succeed straight away. As we all know, practice takes time. Only in taking your practice into your everyday life will you truly reap the benefits from your hard work throughout this book so far.

Level Up

All of the strategies you practised here are the vital components for building your memory palace. In the final chapter, you will add one more skill to your arsenal: the ability to put all of your images, associations and knowledge structures into a three-dimensional environment that you will navigate. This spatial component is the last pillar that makes your memories even more stable. Make sure that you take the opportunity to first use the puzzles in this chapter to hone your powers of visualization, association and organization to aid your memory before you move on to the next level. This will make building your palace a lot easier.

The Fault in Our Memories

Our memories are not set in stone. Over time, they become coarser and lose detail until we may only be able to remember the gist of a movie or a news story. Back in exercise 2.9, you were asked to remember a list of words. First, try to think back to what words were on that list. It is quite difficult with nothing to go on! So let's work with cues instead as we have seen how helpful those can be: was the word Magnesium in the list? How about Platinum? And Helium?

If you said Helium was in the list, you had what is called a false memory. Don't worry, false memories are not uncommon, especially in the case of this exercise where we fiendishly threw in many words that centred around a specific concept (the periodic table)! That is, the words were semantically related. This way of organizing memories into a structure under a common theme can be helpful but it can also lead to blurring of the details. The key is to make these similar items more distinct and more memorable next time.

3.1: Astronomical Awareness

Not all planets of the solar system are orbited by moons, but most are. Take a look at the following list, which shows the largest moon of each planet – if it has one.

First, memorize the list, then see if you can recall it immediately afterwards on a blank piece of paper. Then, try again in an hour, and then tomorrow, the day after and even a few days after that.

Mercury	*No moons*
Venus	*No moons*
Earth	Moon
Mars	Phobos
Jupiter	Ganymede
Saturn	Titan
Uranus	Titania
Neptune	Triton

3.2: Muscle Memory 1

Read this short passage and try to memorize the basic facts:

The human body has approximately 600 muscles, the largest of which is the gluteus maximus. There are three main types of muscle: skeletal, smooth and cardiac. Most muscles are found in pairs. Identical pairs on opposite sides of the body are known as bilateral muscles.

Now cover over the passage, and try to answer the following questions:

1. Approximately how many muscles does the human body have?

2. Which is the largest muscle in the body?

3. What are the three main types of muscle?

4. What name is given to identical muscle pairs on opposite sides fo the body?

Did you remember everything? If not, repeat the exercise until you can answer all four questions successfully.

3.3: Director Directions

The first Oscar for 'Best Director' – more formally known as the 'Academy Award for Best Director' – was awarded by the Academy of Motion Picture Arts and Sciences in 1929.

See how easily you can learn the following list of recent winners of the 'Best Director' Oscar, sorted by the year the award was given. Then, in an hour's time, read the opposite page and try answering the questions.

▶ **2006** *Brokeback Mountain*

▶ **2007** *The Departed*

▶ **2008** *No Country for Old Men*

▶ **2009** *Slumdog Millionaire*

▶ **2010** *The Hurt Locker*

▶ **2011** *The King's Speech*

▶ **2012** *The Artist*

▶ **2013** *Life of Pi*

▶ **2014** *Gravity*

▶ **2015** *Birdman*

▶ **2016** *The Revenant*

▶ **2017** *La La Land*

▶ **2018** *The Shape of Water*

▶ **2019** *Roma*

▶ **2020** *Parasite*

Make sure you have covered the list on the previous page before you attempt this exercise.

Now see how many of the following questions about recent Oscar-winning films for 'Best Director' you can answer:

1. What was the most recent film in the list, for 2020?

2. In what year did *Slumdog Millionaire* win?

3. Which film had the shortest name?

4. Which film was sixth in the list, reading from top to bottom?

5. Which film won in 2007?

6. Which film won the year before *The Shape of Water* won?

7. How many films were in the list in total?

8. Which film won the year after *Birdman* won?

3.4: Muscle Memory 2

Now read this longer passage about muscles, and memorize as many details as you can. You may want to read the passage several times.

The smallest muscles in the body are found in the same place as the smallest bones: the ear. The stapedius is the smallest muscle, at just over 1mm in length, and it helps to control the smallest bone, the stapes.

The longest muscle is the sartorius, which is found in the thigh. Its name comes from the Latin word for 'tailor', supposedly due to the cross-legged position in which tailors sat.

Muscles and bones are attached together with tendons. These are different to ligaments, which attach bones to one another. The Achilles tendon, named after the Greek hero, can be found in the ankle. It is also known as the heel cord.

Once you are happy you'll remember all of the facts above, set a timer for an hour. When the hour is up, read the instructions on the opposite page.

First, cover over the passage on the previous page. Then, how many of the questions below can you successfully answer, based on the information that was given in the passage?

1. Where is the smallest muscle in the body?

2. What is the Achilles tendon also known as?

3. Where is the longest muscle in the body?

4. Which is the smallest bone in the body?

5. Which mythology does the hero Achilles belong to?

6. Which muscle is named after the Latin word for 'tailor'?

7. What type of structure connects bones to other bones?

8. What is the length of the body's smallest muscle?

How much did you recall? Check back to the previous page and repeat the exercise if necessary.

3.5: Lost for Words

Four of the longer words in English have been written below, rotated sideways for space! Can you memorize their spellings? Once you think you've learned them, set a timer for ten minutes. When time is up, continue on the opposite page.

Supercalifragilisticexpialidocious

Antidisestablishmentarianism

Floccinaucinihilipilification

Pneumonoultramicroscopicsilicovolcanoconiosis

Make sure you've studied the list of words on the previous page before you attempt the recall task below.

After you've waited ten minutes, see if you can both remember the four words in their entirety *and* spell each of them correctly on the blank lines below:

....

....

....

....

Did you spell all four correctly? Check back to the opposite page and see how you did.

For an extra challenge, you could test yourself to see if you can both recall and spell them correctly on a blank piece of paper tomorrow morning – without looking at the list again.

3.6: Gold Standard

Take a couple of minutes to memorize this list of recent
Olympic gold medallists in the men's 100m sprint:

Marcell Jacobs (2020)

Usain Bolt (2008, 2012, 2016)

Justin Gatlin (2004)

Maurice Greene (2000)

Donovan Bailey (1996)

Once you're ready, cover over the list and see if you can fill
in the names below, noting that the years are now given in a
different order:

.... **(2000)**

.... **(2004)**

.... **(2020)**

.... **(2008, 2012, 2016)**

.... **(1996)**

3.7: Dates to Remember

Spend up to five minutes studying this list of historical dates:

2nd June 1953: Queen Elizabeth II crowned

2nd March 1969: First Concorde flight

20th July 1969: Man lands on the moon

16th August 1977: Elvis Presley dies

9th November 1989: Berlin Wall falls

26th June 1997: First *Harry Potter* book published

21st March 2006: First tweet sent on Twitter

Once you have memorized the dates and the events that took place on them, set a timer for two hours. After two hours, follow the instructions on the next page.

Now it's time to see how many of the historical dates and their associated events you can recall.

Note that the list below is in a different order to that previously given – i.e. it's no longer in chronological order.

......................................: First tweet sent on Twitter

9th November 1989: ....

2nd March 1969: ....

......................................: Queen Elizabeth II crowned

......................................: Man lands on the moon

......................................: First *Harry Potter* book published

16th August 1977: ....

3.8: Lost and Found 1

Study this list of things which are easily lost. After a few minutes, cover them up and follow the instructions below.

Keys

Time

Glasses

Remote control

Wallet

The plot

Single socks

Sleep

Bank card

Marbles

Once you have covered up the above list, see if you can repeat it aloud to yourself from memory. The first letters of each item are given below to help you, in the same order as they originally appeared:

K T G R W T S S B M

3.9: Lost and Found 2

After the previous exercise, where you memorized a list of easily lost things, why not make your own list to make sure you're never without the essential items you tend to lose? Write your list of often-forgotten items here:

....

....

....

....

....

....

....

Now write the first letter of each item in one of the gaps below. Can you think of a way to link these letters with a mnemonic and commit the list to your long-term memory?

....

3.10: Use Your Imagination

Spend five minutes reading the fictional scenarios below, and really try to picture them happening in your mind's eye.

When you have finished reading the list, cover it up and set a timer for an hour – or longer, if you're feeling brave. When your timer is up, follow the instructions on the next page.

▶ **A pink pigeon steals an ice cream from an enormous red dog**

▶ **A clown's lawnmower keeps blowing bubbles instead of cutting the grass**

▶ **A one-eyed pirate sails a golden ship off the end of the earth**

▶ **A bottomless bowl of popcorn is delivered to a house made of gingerbread**

▶ **The name of a famous cyclist is spelled out in stars across the night sky**

▶ **A school headteacher falls into a giant vat of baked beans**

Make sure you've read the instructions and scenarios on the previous page before you attempt this exercise.

Now try answering the following questions about the fictional scenarios:

1. What kind of sportsperson had their name written in the stars?

2. What was the pirate's ship made of?

3. What colour was the dog that had its ice cream stolen?

4. What was in the bottomless bowl?

5. What was the job of the person who fell into the baked beans?

6. What was the clown's lawnmower doing instead of cutting the grass?

7. Which character had one eye?

8. What was the house made of?

3.11: Sequence of Events

Spend three minutes studying this list of gardening topic headings. You don't need to remember the order they are listed in, but try instead to picture each of the topics clearly in your mind.

Once you're learned the list of headings, read the instructions on the next page.

Preparing the soil

Sowing seeds

Harvesting

Keeping pests at bay

Suitable planting locations

Removing weeds

Thinning seedlings

Cooking your vegetables

Vegetables to plant together

Supporting stalks and stems

Can you now recall all ten gardening headings from the previous page? Can you write them down below, but in a logical way according to how you think they might be ordered on a book's contents page. And if you have trouble recalling them all, try thinking chronologically about how plants grow to see if that jogs your memory. One possible ordering is given on page 191, once you're done.

3.12: Rhyme Time 1

Poems, songs and rhyming words all come in handy when looking for methods to help you memorize lists or important facts. For example, the following rhyming verse is famously helpful for remembering the number of days in each month:

> **Thirty days hath September,**
>
> **April, June and November;**
>
> **All the rest have thirty-one**
>
> **Except for February alone**

The poem works despite the final two lines only half-rhyming, and the fact that 'December' could also complete either of the first two lines while still rhyming. Making up your own rhymes can be a useful memorization method.

Write your own rhyme about the history of the United Kingdom, to help you memorize the following facts:

▶ **The union of England (which included Wales, annexed in 1542) with Scotland in 1707 formed the United Kingdom of Great Britain**

▶ **This later became the United Kingdom of Great Britain and Ireland in 1801, and the United Kingdom of Great Britain and Northern Ireland in 1927**

3.13: Monarchic Memory

See if you can create a rhyming poem to help you memorize the names – and the order of ascension to the throne – of the twelve British monarchs who have reigned since the unification of Great Britain in 1707. The dates are included for information only, and need not be memorized.

Anne	1707 (start of reign)
George I	1714
George II	1727
George III	1760
George IV	1820
William IV	1830
Victoria	1837
Edward VII	1901
George V	1910
Edward VIII	1936
George VI	1936
Elizabeth II	1952

Use the space below to write down your rhyming poem to
help you remember the twelve monarchs. Remember, the
rhyme scheme doesn't have to be perfect – just memorable!

....

....

....

....

....

....

....

....

....

....

Once you've created your poem, put it to the test: reread it
several times, then see if you can still recall it in an hour's
time without looking back at your notes.

3.14: Acrostic Aids

The items in the list below appear, in the order given, in the Christmas carol *The Twelve Days of Christmas*:

Partridge in a pear tree

Turtle doves

French hens

Calling birds

Gold rings

Geese a-laying

Swans a-swimming

Maids a-milking

Ladies dancing

Lords a-leaping

Pipers piping

Drummers drumming

The first five lines are well known, but often the later items in the list become confused with one another and are harder to remember due to their similarities with one another.

Can you create an acrostic-style phrase to help you remember the correct order of items in the list?

Use the space below to create your acrostic aid, using the first letters of each of the items in the list to create a memorable sentence or phrase which includes them all. The list starts at the sixth item, 'geese a-laying'. For ladies and lords you might want to start words with 'la' and 'lo' respectively to help distinguish between them. So, for example, it could be 'God Sends My Lady-Love Plentiful Doughnuts'.

G ....

S ....

M ....

La ....

Lo ....

P ....

D ....

Once you've completed your acrostic, put it to the test: can you still remember the order of the days of Christmas tomorrow? What about next week?

3.15: Blend It Together

Study the list below, which is made up of unrelated facts, words and other items. Using any of the techniques you've used so far for remembering, try to come up with a way to memorize all of the items *and* the order they are listed in.

The Art of Hang-gliding

Mellifluous

10th August 1932: Lego founded

Three octopuses in a string bag

QWERTY4567

***Mamma Mia* by ABBA**

Solar plexus

Elizabeth I

Ice cream, you scream

Alfa, Bravo, Charlie, Delta

Once you think you've successfully memorized both the items on the previous page and their order, cover them up and then see if you can recall all ten of them, in order, on the blank list below.

....

....

....

....

....

....

....

....

How did you do? Try the same challenge again in 24 hours, using a blank piece of paper – taking the time to relearn the list first if you struggled to recall it above.

Then try again in three day's time.

3.16: Test Your Memory

How have you been finding the memorization tasks in this chapter? It's time to find out, since each of the following questions relates to one of the memory exercises in the previous pages. Try to answer them without looking back at the original exercises. If you need them, solutions can be found on page 192.

1. Which is the largest muscle in the body?

2. How many King Edwards were there in the list of monarchs?

3. Who won the gold in the Olympic men's 100m sprint back in 2000?

4. What is the name of Jupiter's largest moon?

5. Which film won the Oscar for 'Best Director' in 2010?

6. Where in the body is the stapedius muscle?

7. Can you fill in the rest of the long English word which had the following first and last letters:

   F..**n**

8. On what date was the first *Harry Potter* book published?

9. What did the pink pigeon steal?

10. Which muscle is named after the Latin word for 'tailor'?

11. Which of these planets does not have a moon?
    ▶ Saturn
    ▶ Venus
    ▶ Neptune

12. You weren't asked to memorize it, but do you remember the year in which the first British monarch took the throne?

Once you've answered all of the questions, try the following challenges. Write your answers on a blank sheet of paper:

▶ **List as many of the titles as you can remember from the list of gardening topics.**
▶ **What are the twelve verses of *The Twelve Days of Christmas*? Can you write them out in day order?**
▶ **Can you write out the names of the twelve British monarchs, listing them in reverse chronological order from Elizabeth II backwards?**

THE MEMORY
PALACE

Stepping into the Palace

He has his eyes closed, a concentrated look on his face. His hands move through the air as if to grasp for objects only to push them away and try again, yet to anyone observing these odd mannerisms it is as if he has lost his mind. But finally, he opens his eyes and the creases between his eyebrows disappear. Sherlock Holmes has emerged from his mind palace with just the information he needs to solve yet another seemingly impenetrable case. This scene, as depicted in the BBC series, illustrates the power that this memory technique holds. Even though it looks like science fiction, it most certainly is better than that: it is science reality. And now that you have taken on various challenges for your short-term and long-term memory and have learned about the basics of remembering, you are ready to do what Sherlock did and take the step into the memory palace.

Ancient Wisdom

The memory palace technique dates back to the great ancient Greek poet Simonides more than 2,500 years ago. It was used by many prominent figures in antiquity to help them memorize long speeches, and by storytellers to recall the many myths and epics that were their stock in trade. And now you can join the ancients by learning this powerful technique.

Memory Grandmasters

Memory grandmasters are not born with their amazing skills. They use techniques that have stood the test of time, with the memory palace being one of the oldest mnemonic devices used around the world.

So, before you begin building your palace, make sure you are not stopped by the very first barrier to your progress: believing that you simply have a bad memory and that's that. You can improve the way you store, retain and retrieve memories, just like Sherlock Holmes, the Greek poets and philosophers did, and memory athletes continue to do today. You just have to learn how to do it!

One Exercise to Rule Them All

A memory palace is a mental map of a place or building in which you use a predefined route to walk from one location to the next while populating each location with an image that represents information you wish to recall. It's a library of sorts which you can walk through in your mind along a set path to visit those places where a given memory is stored.

The memory palace method is so effective because it uses all the skills the hippocampus has to offer while working in a concerted effort with a multitude of other brain regions involved in processing of sensory information, working memory, and even navigation. In this process:

▶ You will draw on your new-found knowledge from previous chapters.

▶ You will use your working memory to keep in mind the scene you are envisioning as you are transferring the new verbal information you are hoping to learn into a visual representation.

▶ You will employ the chunking method of putting together multiple pieces of information into one coherent image.

▶ Searching in your long-term memory, you will use what you already know to form a link to novel information, creating strong associations.

This entire process is one big exercise in elaborative encoding, the strategy by which to-be-remembered information is actively made more memorable as it is laid

Memory Workhorse

Without knowing it, the ancient Greeks designed the memory palace technique in such a way that it taxes all the key functions of the hippocampus: the generation of highly detailed mental images, the forging of associations between multiple pieces of information, the spatial navigation between multiple loci and the consolidation of new memories to ensure they are here to stay.

This is not a coincidence. All of these functions allow the hippocampus to construct a dynamic, adaptive mental map of our environment. By rapidly establishing novel associations the hippocampus embeds our new experiences within the tapestry of our existing knowledge. These hippocampal maps are therefore central to our survival because only by integrating knowledge over time and putting memories into context with each other do we have the tools to react appropriately to new challenges posed by a constantly changing world.

The hippocampus is a team player and a hub of a network of brain regions for long-term memory and navigation. People who use this memory palace technique exhibit altered brain activation and connectivity patterns during memory tasks compared to individuals who are using other ways of remembering. Specifically, the hippocampus becomes more strongly connected to other brain regions in the network that supports recollection and these changes in brain activity are associated with better long-term memory performance. Even after six weeks of training, the pattern of brain activation in those memory networks among former novices became more similar to those found in experienced memory champions, demonstrating the brain's remarkable capacity for learning.

down in your long-term store. You have already come across these types of exercises in smaller forms throughout the previous chapters and are now equipped to build on them.

Focus!

How often do you actively think to yourself, 'I need to remember this later'? After graduating from school or college, we do not typically need to memorize vast amounts of information about a specific topic by heart any more. As a result, when we go about our day, we may not always engage our memory in a mindful, focused manner. We might make a mental note of an item on our to-do list, but much of this can now be done using mnemonic aids as well as apps on your smartphone.

Actively working on forming new memories to remember facts for lack of an alternative has, in many cases, become a thing of the past. And that is where we run into the second potential roadblock: forgetting to set aside some time in which to focus on incorporating a piece of novel information into your palace. You should do this even if you are having a busy day and need to quickly rush off to the next task.

As you may remember from previous chapters, most content in our short-term memory is never made into long-term

memories. Constantly shifting your attention only hampers this process. Setting aside some time to focus on applying the memory palace method in your everyday life will be challenging to begin with but will soon become easier and easier. Even a short period of time helps to keep the ball rolling.

Location, Location, Location!

So, you have decided on committing something to memory but what ingredients does a memory palace need?

First, you need to think of an environment with a set of separate locations that can be used as 'loci' for pieces of information you wish to remember. The environment should be familiar to you, so that conjuring up a mental image of the place can come easily. It could be your house, your office, the grocery store, a train station or your old school building – it does not actually have to be a palace! Anything with distinct but familiar locations will do.

Once the bare bones of the memory palace have been constructed, the next step of the building process consists of choosing your 'loci', a set of locations in your environment. Suitable loci could be a kitchen counter, a fridge, the dinner table or any other locations that could then be connected naturally by a mental walk.

In the next step, you should plan a journey from one virtual locus to the next, defining a fixed path that will guide you through your memory palace. The environment, the loci and the predetermined route between loci function as your foundation: the scaffold for your mental library. This approach of constructing your palace is why the memory palace technique is also known as the 'Method of Loci' or the 'Memory Journey'.

Memory Furniture

Once you can easily picture your memory palace and the journey through its loci, the stage is set and it is time to populate your palace with memories.

Each of the loci serves as a place within your palace at which you can deposit a memory. Starting with a list of information you wish to enshrine in your long-term store, for instance a shopping list, you would follow your memorized defined path between loci by 'walking' from one to the next, each time choosing one item from the list which you transform into a mental image and link to the current location before you continue onwards.

Having defined your scaffold of environment, loci and route before you begin to use it for memorization, you have the advantage of a reduced workload when you begin depositing memories at each locus during your mental walk. Whenever you hope to recall the information, you can retrace your journey from start to finish, each time retrieving what you stored at a given location as you navigate between loci.

This may all sound rather technical, so let's move on to see an example of the method in action!

Getting Started

A Road Map to Memory

For the following exercises, it is easiest if you stick to one familiar environment, like your home, and use the different rooms to deposit your memories.

Let's begin with a simple everyday example: your grocery shopping list. Most of us write down a list of items to buy to ensure that we are not forgetting anything. But, if you use the memory palace technique correctly, you won't need a written list in the future.

First, let's build a palace:

▶ **Step one**

Step one of the construction phase is complete: you have chosen your home as the environment.

▶ **Step two**

Now you must identify the loci. These could be your rooms: your hallway, sitting room, kitchen, bathroom or bedroom may be suitable. If your home does not have as many rooms, you can pick multiple spots within a room, like the different pieces of furniture, or you may choose another building, like your old school.

▶ **Step three**

Finally, you map out your path between loci. You may begin in the hallway, then move to the living room and into your kitchen. Finally, you may arrive in the bedroom. The scaffold is made.

You now take as long as you need to memorize your palace, so that its loci, and the route between them, becomes so familiar that you can recall it without any conscious effort. If your first palace is based on a real-life location, real-life loci and a real-life route then this will be much easier, since much

of the memorization effort will have already been done for you by virtue of simply being able to retrace long-familiar physical footsteps, but now simply within your mind.

Memorizing a palace may seem like a lot of effort to go to simply to build a scaffold for future memorization, but the key thing to understand is that you only build it once. Then, once it is built, you can use it for evermore.

Of course, you may at some point outgrow your palace – and when the moment arrives you can simply extend it, either by adding extra loci or by adding extra rooms. Or, eventually, the day may come to move into a new palace...

Follow the Map

To use your memory palace, you now walk around it on your predetermined route, placing one item you wish to later recall at each locus you come to.

This is where your inner Picasso is needed to paint memorable mental pictures of each item in its location. You should try to make the memory as vivid as you can, adding specific details that make it distinct. Be creative, have fun, conjure up a captivating image or, better yet, a short mental movie. Your imagination is the limit. Tying the new information to something surprising, funny or meaningful to you makes for a unique image, helping you to actively fight interference, that pesky enemy of memory.

Let's say your shopping list is as follows:

Eggplant

Six apples

Yoghurt

Coffee

Chicken

Now let's put them into your palace:

▶ The first image for the eggplant may be a table in the hallway that contains a vase of flowers, in the midst of which you can find the vegetable.

▶ Walking to the living room, you may see a family of six apples bouncing up and down your couch.

▶ Making your way to the kitchen, yoghurt may be spilling from the fridge all over the floor.

▶ As you progress to the bathroom, your bathtub or shower is clogged with coffee grounds.

▶ At the last stop, a loose chicken is running through your bedroom with feathers flying everywhere.

You can also incorporate different sensations into the memory to strengthen it further. You might hear the agitated clucking of the chicken or the excited squeals of the bouncing apples; you might smell the coffee or touch the cold spilled yoghurt. The more vivid these images become, the more likely that the memory will stick! It's elaborative encoding at its best, and combining information from multiple senses such as vision, audio and smell is an effective tool for creating rich, lasting memories.

Repeat the Journey

Finally, at some future point in time when you hope to recall your memorized shopping list, you simply start at the beginning and follow your route.

You begin in your hallway from where you will navigate through your virtual environment from one location to the next, each time observing the scene and retrieving its content.

Each location will act as a cue that can help you recollect the associated information. You have successfully created a roadmap to long-term memory retention and recall!

4.1: Build Your Palace

Have you decided which loci you'll be adding to your
memory palace? Start by making a list of five locations, in the
order that you'll visit them. These could be rooms, or they
could be objects within those rooms.

▶ ....

▶ ....

▶ ....

▶ ....

▶ ....

Now you must memorize a journey that travels through
those five locations, in order. The idea is to make that journey
so familiar that you never have to think about the journey
itself – it's as automatic as remembering your name. In that
way you will always have a reliable memory trigger for every
item you want to memorize.

4.2: Shopping Prep

Use your memory palace to memorize the following list of items. Take as long as you like to try to come up with a strong connection between each locus and the item you need to memorize.

Sandwich

Newspaper

Spaghetti

Tomatoes

Olive oil

Once you are happy you've stored the items in your memory palace, placing one item in the first location, another in the second location, and so on, then cover the list and see how easily you can recall all five items. Then try again in ten minutes – is the list still easy to recall?

4.3: Extend Your Palace

Let's make your palace bigger, adding five further loci so you can store more in it. If you're basing it on a real location then you may not have ten rooms you can use, so in which case you can either attach fictional rooms (how about a throne room?) or link it 'magically' to another location you are familiar with. You can also subdivide rooms by objects within them – so your kitchen might have the table, the fridge, the cooker, and so on, all as separate loci.

Now memorize your journey through all ten rooms. By always travelling the same route you make it easier to remember *all* the locations – and you gain the ability to remember the *order* of a list of items 'for free'.

4.4: *Shopping Again*

In exercise 4.2, you were asked to memorize a list of five
items. See how you do now by adding five further items onto
the list, to make the following list of ten items in total:

Sandwich
Newspaper
Spaghetti
Tomatoes
Olive oil
Milk
Orange juice
Yoghurt
Cornflakes
Doughnuts

Once you're happy you'll remember all ten items, cover the
book and see if you can write them all on a blank piece of
paper. Repeat the exercise until you can memorize them all.

4.5: *Tall Tales*

Listed below are the names of eight characters from the children's book *The Wind in the Willows*, listed in a particular (although otherwise meaningless) order. See how quickly you can memorize this list of eight characters – and their ordering – in your memory palace.

Mole
Otter
Mr Badger
Pan
The Gaoler's Daughter
Ratty
Mr Toad
Portly

Once you're confident you've learned this ordered list, cover over this page and see if you can recall them on a separate piece of paper, simply by walking through your memory palace.

4.6: Scaling New Heights

Take as long as you need to memorize this list of the world's tallest mountain peaks, listed in order of decreasing height above sea level:

Mount Everest

K2

Kangchenjunga

Lhotse

Makalu

Cho Oyu

Dhaulagiri I

Manaslu

Nanga Parbat

Annapurna I

Once you think you've memorized the list, cover it up and set a timer for 30 minutes. Once time is then up, can you write out the full list in the same order given above?

Expanding Your Palace

Let's say that you want to use your palace to memorize your grocery list. If so, it will probably contain more than just ten items so you'll want to expand your palace further still.

Perhaps the best way to do this is to increase the number of loci in each room by anchoring information to different pieces of furniture, which for ease of recall you may wish to visit by travelling around the room in a clockwise fashion.

Ordering Techniques

When memorizing an unordered list, such as a grocery list, it is frequently helpful to place related items – such as those items that you will find close to one another in the grocery store – into the same room. A mental walk between different loci feels more natural, and you will have the benefit of a strong sense as to which room belongs to which concepts. And – in the particular case of groceries – if you add the items to your cart in the order you recall them, it will make your shopping trip considerably simpler, saving you from having to repeatedly criss-cross through the store while following the journey in your mind.

4.7: Memory Challenges

See if you can use any of your existing memory techniques to memorize each of these short lists of more complex items. For each set of items, try breaking the individual words or strings down into smaller, more memorable 'chunks' to help you remember them. It's a technique you may already use when learning phone numbers – or unusual words!

List 1 – Welsh Words

Study this list of words and their translations until you are confident you'll recall them. Then cover the words and see if you can rewrite them all in the spaces below.

rhyngwladwriaethol   international
camddealltwriaeth   misunderstanding
anghyfansoddiadol   unconstitutional
llongyfarchiadau   congratulations

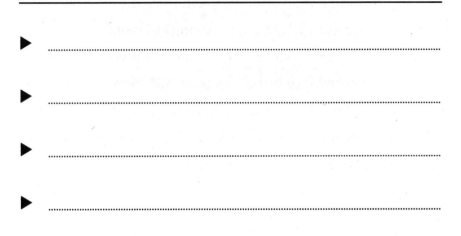

List 2 – Long Numbers

See if you can memorize these two long numbers. Can you later recall them on a blank piece of paper?

2648024640624
6593750573051

List 3 – Complex Codes

Study these two arbitrary codes for as long as it takes you to memorize them. Once you're ready, cover over the codes and see if you can write them out on a blank piece of paper.

UD30LGN4894H
8403NF9J2LDJR

4.8: Further Enlargement

If you haven't already, extend your palace further so that it now has at least fifteen loci. At some point, of course, you may wish to start a new palace – memory masters can have many different palaces, some of which may also be tailored for memorizing different types of information.

Now try memorizing this list of fifteen items:

Magazine
Armchair
Zebra
Steering wheel
Fireplace
Laptop
Airport
Bath mat
Gardening tools
Dictionary
Stepladder
Koala
Feather
Pasta
Tape measure

4.9: Time to Pack

Spend several minutes memorizing this list of things to pack for a holiday:

Card games

Sunglasses

Passport

Sunscreen

Swimwear

Towels

Reading book

Foreign currency

Notebook

First-aid kit

Tickets

Travel guide

When you think you've studied the list for long enough, set a timer for an hour and cover up the list.

When the hour is up, see if you can recall all of the items and the order they were given. How many did you remember?

4.10: An Alternative Palace

Listed below are a number of rooms which you might find in a memory palace, and one item to place in each of them. Using this list of rooms – instead of your own palace – see if you can store all ten items. The 'palace' is listed again at the bottom of the page, so see if you can then recall all ten items from this new palace journey.

Porch	Umbrella
Hallway	Dog
Basement	Toolbox
Kitchen	Phone
Living room	Pillow
Dining room	Chocolates
Bedroom	Onions
Bathroom	Laptop computer
Staircase	Dictionary
Utility room	Cheese

Once you are ready, cover over the list above and see if you can travel through the palace – given below – and recall all ten items.

Porch	**Hallway**	**Basement**
Kitchen	**Living room**	**Dining room**
Bedroom	**Bathroom**	**Staircase**
	Utility room	

Taking It to the Next Level

In your next exercise, you will be asked to remember the capital cities of certain countries around the world. You can reuse the same loci you previously used for your shopping example or you may decide to choose entirely new ones – or even a separate environment. Now the challenge is to turn the names of countries and cities into mental images. This is likely to be more difficult than the shopping list example because of the more abstract nature of the content you hope to recall.

Example Loci

Using your bathroom as an example, two of your loci may be the bathtub and the sink.

▶ For 'Turkey' and 'Ankara', you could picture yourself pulling up an anchor with a turkey from your bathtub. This strategy of tying unfamiliar words to images of similarly sounding familiar objects provides a useful memory aid for a visualization of the novel, abstract content.

▶ For 'Chile' and 'Santiago', you may think of the parrot Iago from the Disney movie *Aladdin* searching for a chilli in a pile of sand in the bathroom sink you walked to after

having discovered the turkey. Again, ridiculous, but the stranger and more unexpected the image, the more likely it is that you can retrieve the memory later on. Every piece in this memory chunk – the parrot, the chilli and the sand – can all serve as a cue to remind you of the full scene and, ultimately, the piece of knowledge you hope to recall.

If you wanted to take this exercise to the next level, you could further structure your memory journey by placing country-city pairs from the same continent into the same room.

Once you have spent some time on this exercise you may find that this new technique improves your ability to recall the countries and cities as compared to your earlier attempts. Drawing on multiple functions at which our brains excel – such as mental imagery, associations and spatial navigation – will have done the trick. And if you notice having forgotten some pairs as you walked between loci, revise the image to ensure better retention next time.

4.11: Capital Cities

Try to memorize this list of fifteen countries and their capital cities. There is no need to recall the exact order of the list, so you can rearrange it as works best for you if you choose to memorize it using your memory palace.

Chile:	Santiago
Costa Rica:	San José
Ecuador:	Quito
Fiji:	Suva
Ghana:	Accra
Lithuania:	Vilnius
Malta:	Valletta
Nigeria:	Abuja
Tanzania:	Dodoma
Pakistan:	Islamabad
Sudan:	Khartoum
Swaziland:	Mbabane
Slovenia:	Ljubljana
Turkey:	Ankara
Uzbekistan:	Tashkent

Once you have memorized the list, try covering over the right-hand side and seeing if you can recall the capital cities when given the country. Then try the reverse – can you also recall the country when given its capital city?

4.12: Language and Memory

Can you use your new skills to memorize this list of words which all mean 'memory' in other languages? Spend as long as you need studying the list, then cover it up.

French:	mémoire
Spanish:	memoria
Norwegian:	hukommelse
Swahili:	kumbukumbu
Polish:	pamięć
Welsh:	cof
Slovenian:	spomin
Irish:	cuimhne
Hawaiian:	ho'omana'o
Samoan:	manatua

With the list covered, see if you can now recall the list of words for 'memory' in all ten different languages. The first letter of each language has been given below to help you, although the letters have been sorted into alphabetical order:

F H I N P S S S W

4.13: Minor Planets

When you were younger, you may have learned an acrostic phrase to help you memorize the order of the planets in our solar system. But what about minor planets?

Listed below are the twenty largest asteroids (all minor planets, except Ceres which is a dwarf planet) found in the asteroid belt between Mars and Jupiter, sorted in decreasing order of diameter*. Some of the names you may recognize, while others may be completely new. Study the list below for as long as you need, until you feel you can remember all of the items. You may want to return to the list a few times in order to memorize it fully, taking breaks in between.

1. Ceres
2. Vesta
3. Pallas
4. Hygiea
5. Interamnia
6. Europa
7. Davida
8. Sylvia
9. Eunomia
10. Euphrosyne
11. Patientia
12. Juno
13. Cybele
14. Bamberga
15. Thisbe
16. Fortuna
17. Psyche
18. Herculina
19. Doris
20. Eugenia

* If including asteroids out to the edge of Neptune's orbit, then position 12 would be occupied by Hektor, a Jupiter trojan. The other two dwarf planets, Pluto and Eris, are both found outside Neptune's orbit.

4.14: Minor Information

Previously you learned the names of the twenty largest asteroids in the asteroid belt. Now spend some time studying information on each of the first four of them. There's no immediate recall exercise for this list, but you will be asked about it in a later exercise.

1. Ceres is the largest asteroid in the solar system, and is named after the Roman goddess of agriculture. It has a diameter of 939km and is designated a dwarf planet.

2. Vesta is the brightest asteroid in the night sky. It was discovered in 1807 and makes up approximately nine per cent of the mass of the asteroid belt.

3. Pallas was an alternative name for the Greek goddess, Athene. The asteroid Pallas has an unusual orbit which would make it tricky to visit via space travel.

4. Hygiea is almost perfectly spherical and is the furthest from the sun of the 'big four' asteroids (that is, the first four on the list). It is named after the Greek goddess for health, whose name also gives us the word 'hygiene'.

4.15: Capital Associations

You may already know the names of all fifty US states – but if you don't, now's the time to learn! Listed below are the names of all of the states *and* their capitals. Study the list for as long as you need, using your favourite techniques to memorize as many as possible. You might want to come back to the list several times in order to cement your learning. Once you are done, write some prompts to test yourself.

▶ **Alabama** – Montgomery   ▶ **Idaho** – Boise

▶ **Alaska** – Juneau   ▶ **Illinois** – Springfield

▶ **Arizona** – Phoenix   ▶ **Indiana** – Indianapolis

▶ **Arkansas** – Little Rock   ▶ **Iowa** – Des Moines

▶ **California** – Sacramento   ▶ **Kansas** – Topeka

▶ **Colorado** – Denver   ▶ **Kentucky** – Frankfort

▶ **Connecticut** – Hartford   ▶ **Louisiana** – Baton Rouge

▶ **Delaware** – Dover   ▶ **Maine** – Augusta

▶ **Florida** – Tallahassee   ▶ **Maryland** – Annapolis

▶ **Georgia** – Atlanta   ▶ **Massachusetts** – Boston

▶ **Hawaii** – Honolulu   ▶ **Michigan** – Lansing

- **Minnesota** – Saint Paul
- **Mississippi** – Jackson
- **Missouri** – Jefferson City
- **Montana** – Helena
- **Nebraska** – Lincoln
- **Nevada** – Carson City
- **New Hampshire** – Concord
- **New Jersey** – Trenton
- **New Mexico** – Santa Fe
- **New York** – Albany
- **North Carolina** – Raleigh
- **North Dakota** – Bismarck
- **Ohio** – Columbus
- **Oklahoma** – Oklahoma City
- **Oregon** – Salem
- **Pennsylvania** – Harrisburg
- **Rhode Island** – Providence
- **South Carolina** – Columbia
- **South Dakota** – Pierre
- **Tennessee** – Nashville
- **Texas** – Austin
- **Utah** – Salt Lake City
- **Vermont** – Montpelier
- **Virginia** – Richmond
- **Washington** – Olympia
- **West Virginia** – Charleston
- **Wisconsin** – Madison
- **Wyoming** – Cheyenne

4.16: Unusual Vocabulary

Can you memorize the following list of thirteen unusual words, and their associated definitions? You may find them tricky to learn, so you'll have to put your best memory skills to the test!

Once you're done, turn the page and see if you can answer the given questions.

ANGUILLIFORM
having the shape of an eel

QUIRE
25 sheets of paper; a twentieth of a ream

YARBOROUGH
a hand of cards where no card is higher than a 9

OCTOTHORP
the symbol '#'

AGELAST
a person who never laughs

PERISTERONIC

relating to pigeons

BORBORYGMUS

stomach rumbling

FUNAMBULIST

a tightrope walker

ORTANIQUE

hybrid between an orange and a tangerine

RUBIGINOUS

rust-coloured

SESQUIPEDALIAN

tending to use long words; long-winded

TRISKAIDEKAPHOBIA

fear of the number 13

INCUNABULUM

a book printed before 1501

Make sure you have memorized the list of unusual words on the previous two pages first. Then, can you fill in the unusual words next to their definitions? Note that the prompts are provided in a different order to the previous page.

relating to pigeons

....

a book printed before 1501

....

having the shape of an eel

....

a tightrope walker

....

rust-coloured

....

tending to use long words; long-winded

....

a person who never laughs

hybrid between an orange and a tangerine

stomach rumbling

fear of the number 13

25 sheets of paper; a twentieth of a ream

a hand of cards where no card is higher than a 9

the symbol '#'

4.17: Capital Recall

In puzzle 4.15, you studied a list of all fifty US states along with their state capitals. How well can you remember them?

Firstly, see if you can remember the first ten states and their capitals, alphabetically, when their initial letters are given:

▶ A.. ....

▶ A.. ....

▶ A.. ....

▶ A.. ....

▶ C.. ....

▶ C.. ....

▶ C.. ....

▶ D.. ....

▶ F ....

▶ G.. ....

Secondly, can you recall the two-word state capitals which begin with the following pairs of initials?

DM   BR   JC   CC   SF   OC

Can you recall which states these cities are the capital of?

▶ **Albany:** ....

▶ **Augusta:** ....

▶ **Honolulu:** ....

▶ **Lincoln:** ....

▶ **Nashville:** ....

▶ **Salem:** ....

▶ **Topeka:** ....

▶ **Trenton:** ....

And can you recall the capital cities for each of these states?

▶ **Wyoming:** ....

▶ **Virginia:** ....

▶ **Maryland:** ....

▶ **Idaho:** ....

▶ **Florida:** ....

▶ **Montana:** ....

▶ **Utah:** ....

▶ **Ohio:** ....

Now turn back to page 164 to see how well you did.

4.18: A Different Breed

Now that your memory palace is firm in your mind, see if
you can use it to remember this list of 28 dog breeds.

Study the words below for as long as you need. Once you've
memorized the list, cover it up and follow the instructions on
the opposite page.

Afghan	**Kelpie**
Beagle	**Labrador**
Boxer	**Mastiff**
Bulldog	**Pinscher**
Chihuahua	**Pointer**
Cocker spaniel	**Pomeranian**
Collie	**Poodle**
Dachshund	**Pug**
Dalmatian	**Retriever**
Foxhound	**Schnauzer**
Great Dane	**Setter**
Greyhound	**Sheepdog**
Husky	**Spitz**
Jack Russell	**Terrier**

With the list covered, can you recall the names of all 28 dog breeds from the list? Fill in the gaps below with the names of the breeds, where the final letter of each word has been given for verification purposes. The two lists are in the same order.

...................................n	...................................e
...................................e	...................................r
...................................r	...................................f
...................................g	...................................r
...................................a	...................................r
...................................l	...................................n
...................................e	...................................e
...................................d	...................................g
...................................n	...................................r
...................................d	...................................r
...................................e	...................................r
...................................d	...................................g
...................................y	...................................z
...................................l	...................................r

4.19: Shakespearean Sonnet

The exercises in this chapter so far have focused on individual items – both familiar and unusual – and using your memory palace to commit these items to memory. But what about a written passage? Spend as long as you feel you need studying the following sonnet by William Shakespeare. Once you think it's committed to memory, cover the poem and follow the instructions on the opposite page.

Shall I compare thee to a summer's day?
Thou art more lovely and more temperate:
Rough winds do shake the darling buds of May,
And summer's lease hath all too short a date:
Sometime too hot the eye of heaven shines,
And often is his gold complexion dimm'd;
And every fair from fair sometime declines,
By chance or nature's changing course untrimm'd;
But thy eternal summer shall not fade
Nor lose possession of that fair thou owest;
Nor shall Death brag thou wander'st in his shade,
When in eternal lines to time thou growest:
    So long as men can breathe or eyes can see,
    So long lives this and this gives life to thee.

With the sonnet on the opposite page covered up, see if you can answer the following questions:

1. How many lines did the sonnet have?

2. Which month is mentioned?

3. How many times is the word 'summer' used?

4. Which words rhymed with the following words, each found at the end of a line?
   ▶ see
   ▶ shines
   ▶ fade
   ▶ owest

5. What is the final line of the sonnet?

Now see if you can recite the entire sonnet from memory.

Try again tomorrow, in a week, in a fortnight, and perhaps even in a month's time. Can you still remember the sonnet?

4.20: More Poetic Power

In the previous chapter, you created your own poem to help you remember a list of recent British monarchs. A limerick by Edward Lear also demonstrated how lists can be incorporated into memorable poems – particularly silly ones.

Limericks are relatively easy to remember, with a predictable rhyme scheme. See if you can write a limerick about owls that includes some or all of the following information:

▶ **Owls are nocturnal, meaning they are active at night**

▶ **There are two main groups of owl: true owls and barn owls**

▶ **Young owls are known as owlets**

▶ **A group of owls is known as a parliament**

▶ **The elf owl is considered to be the world's smallest owl**

▶ **Owls have eye 'tubes' instead of eyeballs, which do not move in their sockets – so owls can only look straight ahead (although they can turn their heads!)**

As a reminder of the structure of limericks, here is another one by Edward Lear:

There was an old man of Dumbree,
Who taught little owls to drink tea;
For he said, "To eat mice is not proper or nice,"
That amiable man of Dumbree.

Now create your own limerick:

....

....

....

....

4.21: Comprehensive Reading

The passage below is an extract from a letter in Mary Shelley's *Frankenstein*. Read it through once, trying to take in as many details as possible and committing as much as you can to memory. Once done, cover it over and follow the instructions on the opposite page.

To Mrs. Saville, England.

St. Petersburgh, Dec. 11th, 17—.

You will rejoice to hear that no disaster has accompanied the commencement of an enterprise which you have regarded with such evil forebodings. I arrived here yesterday, and my first task is to assure my dear sister of my welfare and increasing confidence in the success of my undertaking.

I am already far north of London, and as I walk in the streets of Petersburgh, I feel a cold northern breeze play upon my cheeks, which braces my nerves and fills me with delight. Do you understand this feeling? This breeze, which has travelled from the regions towards which I am advancing, gives me a foretaste of those icy climes. Inspirited by this wind of promise, my daydreams become more fervent and vivid. I try in vain to be persuaded that the pole is the seat of frost and desolation; it ever presents itself to my imagination as the region of beauty and delight.

With the passage on the opposite page covered up, see if you can answer the questions below:

1. Who was the letter addressed to?

2. What was the date on the letter?

3. Which country was the letter sent to?

4. When did the writer arrive in their new surroundings?

5. What was the 'first task' that the writer undertook when they arrived?

6. What do you think the relationship is between the writer and the recipient?

7. Which city does the writer say they were 'far north' of?

8. The writer asks their recipient a single question in the letter. What is that question?

9. In the final line of the passage, how does the writer describe the North Pole in their imagination?

4.22: The Name Game

If you feel that you're now an experienced memory palace user, you could try stretching yourself. With practice, you can minimize the amount of time it takes you to place each item into your palace.

As a test, spend no more than five to ten minutes memorizing the list of names below, using whichever techniques you feel work best for you. When time is up, cover the list.

▶	Mary	▶	Sian
▶	Sam	▶	Dinah
▶	Juan	▶	Raoul
▶	Isla	▶	Asher
▶	Phoebe	▶	Beatrice
▶	Priti	▶	Micah
▶	Mina	▶	Ali
▶	Ajax	▶	Poppy
▶	Sophia	▶	Briony
▶	Finn	▶	Mo
▶	Ana	▶	Lukasz
▶	Izaak	▶	Merida

How many of the names can you now recall?

4.23: Practice Makes Perfect

In this final memorization task, give yourself just ten minutes to memorize the list below, using the memory palace technique.

A photo frame
A desk lamp
A loaf of bread
A lawnmower
A deck of cards
A potted plant
A roll of sticky tape
A set of car keys
A pair of socks
A sewing machine
A calculator
A laundry basket
A trampoline
A single shoelace
An alarm clock
A pencil sharpener
An umbrella
A tube of toothpaste
A pair of earrings

See if you can recall the whole list at this time tomorrow.

4.24: Test Your Memory

How much do you remember of the various exercises in this
chapter? Each of the following questions relates to one of
the memorization tasks in this chapter. See how many you
can answer without checking back to the original exercises –
and find out which memories have stuck! If you need them,
solutions to these ten questions can be found on page 192.

1. What is the Welsh word for 'congratulations'?

2. Which asteroid is the brightest in the night sky?

3. Which is the fifth-highest mountain peak in the world?

4. What is the state capital of Maine?

5. Which word means 'having the shape of an eel'?

6. What is the Slovenian word for 'memory'?

7. Which owl is considered the world's smallest?

8. How many names from the list in exercise 4.22 began
   with the letter 'M'?

9. There were thirteen unusual words in a list earlier in this chapter, but which one specifically referenced the number thirteen?

10. Which two characters from *The Wind in the Willows* were the last two in the ordered list?

Once you've answered these questions, see how many of the following challenges you can complete, writing your answers on blank sheets of paper:

▶ What were the ten items in the full shopping list at the start of this chapter? (Exercise 4.4)

▶ Which items did you take to pack on holiday? (Exercise 4.9)

▶ How many of the twenty largest asteroids in the asteroid belt can you remember the names of? (Exercise 4.13)

▶ How many of the dog breeds can you recall? (Exercise 4.18)

▶ Can you still recite the Shakespearean sonnet from memory? (Exercise 4.19)

▶ How many everyday items from the final list in exercise 4.23 can you recall?

▶ Can you remember all ten words for 'memory' in different languages – and which language each belongs to? (Exercise 4.12)

4.25: The Ultimate Test

See if you can answer the following questions and complete the various challenges, which will ask you to recall information from across the whole book.

▶ What is the name of this person?

▶ Can you list the five films which won the Oscar for 'Best Picture' from 2000 to 2004?

▶ How many items can you recall from the shopping list where they all began with the letter 's'?

▶ How many of the jokes can you still remember the set-up and punchline of?

▶ In approximately what year did Leonardo da Vinci draw *The Vitruvian Man*?

▶ Which of the words of Japanese origin can you still recall?

▶ What is the name of Neptune's largest moon?

▶ How many films can you remember from the list of 'Best Director' Oscar winners?

▶ What is the Achilles tendon also known as?

▶ Which five athletes won the men's 100m sprint at the 1996 to 2020 Olympic games?

▶ What was the full date of Concorde's first flight?

▶ How many of the topic headings can you remember from the 'gardening' list?

▶ Can you name the twelve most recent British monarchs, starting with Elizabeth II and working backwards?

▶ Can you name all the gifts in the song *The Twelve Days of Christmas*, and the order in which they are given?

▶ Can you write out all four of the Welsh words you learned, and their translations?

▶ Can you name the ten highest mountain peaks in the world, in order from largest to smallest?

▶ How many of the fifty US states *and* their capitals can you still recall?

▶ How many of the thirteen 'unusual' English words can you successfully remember – and their definitions?

▶ Can you recite the 'owl' limerick you created?

You'll have to check back through the book for answers to the above questions, but if you can make headway on more than just a few of the tasks above then you absolutely deserve huge congratulations – you're now a memory palace master!

The Final Word

If you made it to this point, you can be proud of yourself!
You have completed many mental exercises and even read
about the science behind the strategies that help you master
them. Now the final challenge is to take your practice to the
'meta' level: memorising facts about memory. Many of the
complex topics that have been introduced to you are quite
abstract and can therefore easily slip your mind in the future.

With the memory palace technique, you can now try to
prevent this from happening. You can begin to organize the
information from the introductory chapter into a memory
palace: there is the hippocampus, our seahorse that you could
picture in a fish tank holding the key to your memory, while
the subway map could remind you of the organisation of our
brain into different networks. The possibilities are endless
and even if you find it difficult to think of engaging images
at first, with practice you will soon let your imagination
run wild with mental pictures that can hold all kinds of
information. Memory grandmasters often have dozens, if
not hundreds, of different memory palaces at their disposal
and if you keep the ball rolling, you will soon have your own
sizeable collection of memory real estate.

SOLUTIONS

Solutions

Solutions are provided only for those exercises where the answer may not be immediately apparent simply by looking back at the first part of the memorization task.

1.10: Picture Arrangement

The changed images are as follows:

1.16: Remember the Difference

The differences are as follows:

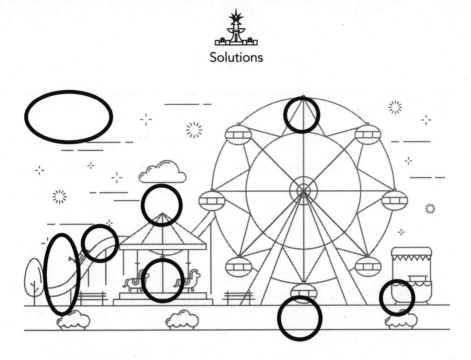

1.17: Added Images

The added images are as follows:

1.18: Vanished Images

The removed images are as follows:

2.11: Spot the Difference

Words that have been changed or removed between the first
and second passages are marked in *italics* below:

It is a truth universally acknowledged, that a *single* man in possession of a *great* fortune, must be in want of a wife.

However little known the feelings or views of such a man may be on his first entering a *community*, this truth is so well fixed in the minds of the surrounding families, that he is considered the rightful property of some one or other of their daughters.

"My dear Mr. Bennet," said his lady to him *yesterday*, "have you heard that *Mansfield* Park is let at last?"

Mr. Bennet replied that he had not.

"But it is," returned she; "for Mrs. *Short* has just been here, and she told me all about it."

Mr. Bennet made no *reply*.

"Do you not want to know who has taken it?" cried his wife *eagerly*.

"You *mean* to tell me, and I have no objection to hearing it."

This was *encouragement* enough.

2.15: Test Your Memory

1. Italy
2. 1772
3. Mr and Mrs Bennet
4. 7112

5. 'Nice belt'

6. Dorset

7. *Gladiator*

8. Clint Eastwood

9. GREEN247

10. There were eight birds: two owls, a hen, four larks and a wren

11. 'Why can't a nose be twelve inches long?'

12. In the order given, the elements were: phosphorous, cobalt, platinum, nickel, magnesium, hydrogen, oxygen, and barium

3.11: Sequence of Events

One possible ordering is as follows:

▶ Vegetables to plant together
▶ Suitable planting locations
▶ Preparing the soil
▶ Sowing seeds
▶ Keeping pests at bay
▶ Thinning seedlings
▶ Supporting stalks and stems
▶ Removing weeds
▶ Harvesting
▶ Cooking your vegetables

3.16: Test Your Memory

1. Gluteus maximus
2. Two
3. Maurice Greene
4. Ganymede
5. *The Hurt Locker*
6. The ear
7. Floccinaucinihilipilification
8. 26th June 1997
9. An ice cream (from the red dog)
10. Sartorius
11. Venus
12. 1707

4.24: Test Your Memory

1. Llongyfarchiadau
2. Vesta
3. Makalu
4. Augusta
5. Anguilliform
6. Spomin
7. The elf owl
8. Five: Mary, Mina, Micah, Mo and Merida
9. Triskaidekaphobia
10. Mr Toad and Portly